# to africa
## with love

# to africa with love

## A Bush Doc's Story

**James Foulkes, M.D.**
WITH Joe Lacy

FRANCIS ASBURY PRESS
*of Evangel Publishing House*
Nappanee, Indiana 46550

Evangel Publishing House
P.O. Box 189
2000 Evangel Way
Nappanee, IN 46550

Toll-Free Order Line: (800) 253-9315
Internet Website: www.evangelpublishing.com

Printed in the United States of America

12          11                                    4          5          6

Originally published by Providence House Publishers, Franklin, Tennessee 37067.
1st printing 2005.
2nd printing 2006, by Evangel Press, Nappanee, Indiana 46550.
3rd printing 2009, by Evangel Press, Nappanee, Indiana 46550.

*Cover illustrations by Juliet Baker*
*Cover design by Joey McNair*

To God, my Father; Jesus Christ, my Savior;
and the Holy Spirit, my Comforter and Guide;
for blessing me with a foreign missionary calling and
empowering me and sustaining me to complete the course.

To my dear wife, Martha, and our three daughters
and their families, who gave encouragement
and advice for this family project.

To our support team who, by their faithful prayers,
financial gifts, and love, allowed us to spend
thirty-eight years in Zambia.

# Contents

# Foreword

Jim Foulkes has lived a full life, an exciting life. And, Jim Foulkes has lived a life of great sacrifice in comparison to the vast community of doctors who practice medicine in the United States. He certainly has not lived in a gated community overlooking a rolling golf course. His life has been a life of heartache and joy, mixed with more than an average share of adventure. Most of all, his life has been one of satisfaction and fulfillment . . . living a life in obedience to his Lord and Savior Jesus Christ. His life exemplifies great service to the One great Master.

God has used this remarkable man in unique ways. Each chapter contained in *To Africa With Love* overflows with emotion and the evident power of God's Holy Spirit working in and through Jim as he faithfully and joyfully served the King of Kings and Lord of Lords. In this book Jim shares the triumphs of missionary medicine, but most of all he shares the power of God working in the hearts of those who populate the dark corners of the African continent.

As you pick up this book to start reading one evening, be prepared for a very long night because you won't be able to put it down until the end. You're in for a treat, you're in for a blessing, and you will be challenged to the depth of your soul.

*Franklin Graham*
President and CEO
Samaritan's Purse
Billy Graham Evangelistic Association

# Acknowledgments

This book would not have been written were it not for the long and continuous urgings of Joe Lacy. After his visit to Mukinge, this book became part of his mind and heart—but not *mine*. My response to Joe was always that there were already enough missionary biographies and the best ones have already been written by the pioneers who came a generation before me.

Just prior to retirement, however, I was challenged by a statement in a book for retiring missionaries: "During your missionary career God did a lot of wonderful things for you, it is now your responsibility to share those things with others."

That hit home, so I started sending some of my yarns to Joe. He and his wife, Winkie, spent many hours picking and choosing from my unrelated stories, improving them, and shaping them into chapters. We then agreed that it would be wise to send the manuscript to a finishing editor.

Enter Jim Adams, a dear friend from Ohio State University days who, with his wife Phyllis, followed our lives in Africa closely as supporters and prayer partners. Jim also visited us at Mukinge, so he is a true insider who walked through our joys and sorrows with us. He was an editor of the *Cincinnati Post* for most of his career and has published three books. Jim undertook the task of being the finishing editor and ended up doing a major rewrite. It was a labor of love in which Jim invested untold hours.

At this point our family became involved in the project and our son-in-law, Ian Caisley, accepted the responsibility of examining the entire manuscript, making suggestions and corrections, and adding two chapters. Thank you, Ian, for adding your highly developed literary talent.

Our dear friend and missionary colleague at Mukinge, Juliet Baker, designed and painted the cover art. Her love for Africa comes through clearly in her important contribution to the book.

The events chosen for the book are selective, thereby passing over many people who were very important in the ministry of Mukinge Hospital in our era. Thanks to those listed here who were important friends and coworkers for at least ten years but do not appear in the events selected for inclusion in the book: Phyllis Spahr Beatty, Ellen Groh, Jan Matthews, Joan Tresidder, Marie Collins, Ken and Cathy Reimer, and Lynn Hacker.

Mukinge was often complimented as having the best lab in a rural hospital in all of Zambia. Thanks to medical technologists: Corrie Hubert, Margaret Watson, Judy Wadge, and Sheila Jubb. The names of our dear faithful Zambian coworkers would fill several pages. Their Lord will reward them for their committed service.

Thanks to Andrew Miller of Providence Publishing Corporation as the initial publisher of this book – with special appreciation to Nancy Wise, the managing editor of PPC, for her friendship and expert final touches to the book. Many thanks to Harold Burgess and The Francis Asbury Society for arranging the second printing through the excellent services of Evangel Press.

World Medical Mission (WMM), a branch of Samaritan's Purse, provided short-term doctors for Mukinge for many years. These doctors gave up their annual holiday to come for a month or so at their own expense, often enabling the career doctors to have a much-needed break. Thanks to that long list of wonderful doctors who helped us. Those committed physicians and their families were a great encouragement and help to us long-termers.

*Jim Foulkes*

Much thanks to the diligent "Mike Wazowski" editorial eye of Madelyn Lacy, my beloved wife. I thank God that in His loving care, He gave you to Coleman, Bennett, and me.

*Joe Lacy*

# Introduction

Daddy wanted his girls to be tough. It stood to reason, because living in Africa demanded that one acquire a certain hardiness. One time we stopped at a friend's farm in Livingstone. The farmer offered to get some workers to retrieve our luggage from the roof rack and carry it in. "Oh no, I'll just have the lads do it," Daddy said, meaning his little hundred-pound girls.

My father would load up the fishing poles for the Lufupa River in Kafue National Park. The silver barbel knew nothing about the wiles of men and we'd catch them with nearly every cast. Daddy expected us to clean any fish caught and retrieve snagged lures. Whining or wimping? Not an option.

One day the mission received a bright orange Dodge truck that we christened the "Big Orange." We took the Big Orange out, and it didn't take long on her maiden voyage to realize our molars were at risk of being jarred loose. Bounced and jolted with every blip on the road, Daddy cheered us on. "It rides hard, gang, and that's the beauty of it." The Big Orange served the mission well for many years, and her hulk can still be seen at Mukinge to this day, housing Auntie Doraine's chickens.

It took a lot to throw Daddy. Once we sliced into a loaf of town-baked supa bread and found a little pink color in every slice, which turned out to be toilet paper. Daddy's response? "Don't worry, honey, it's only slightly used."

Daddy was a "hail friend, well met!" kind of person and the latch on our door was always open to a parade of travelers. Thanks to Mom and Dad, they made sure we traveled some ourselves and gathered some of the most wonderful family memories. We recall: Traveling through then-Rhodesia with the Frews, gliding through the heathery moors of the Eastern highlands and on to Mozambique and Beira. Camping along the white sand banks of the Kabompo River (an economical—if not exciting—alternative to staying at home on holiday when funds were low). Watching huge herds of elephants lumber across the river, the herd keeping a nervous eye on us, and vice versa. Keeping a spotter atop the riverbank to watch for crocs slithering into the water. Collecting fresh clams and cooking fresh antelope. Having a fine book read aloud after supper, only to be interrupted by an angry hippo splashing and snorting, furious that it was caught momentarily on our night fishing line (about the only action that occurred on the fishing line that night).

Daddy made it to Sakeji (our boarding school) when he could, excitedly cheering us on at the school races. In first grade, my sister Gwennie was the fastest girl and Don Amborski was the fastest boy. Many years later, Don would catch up with Gwen and ask her to marry him.

During the rains, one of our traditions was to jaunt off into the bush to hunt mushrooms. We'd get up before sunrise, pack lunch, and drive off into the bush. Some of the mushrooms were as large as umbrellas. After collecting our share of the edible mushrooms, we'd build a fire and cook our meal.

My father was very careful in the operating room, and that thoroughness carried over with preparations the night before a hunting trip. Like a high priest performing rites, he meticulously oiled his gun to perfection, using lubricant made from the tail of a monitor lizard. I remember the lingering smell of that oil on my father and always wished someone would make a manly aftershave based on that wonderful scent.

I once thanked Daddy for all the exciting, adventurous times we'd experienced growing up. He gave me a shy look and said in his self-effacing way, "Well, I just took you along to do all the things I enjoyed doing."

Daddy was hardly ever sick, but once he developed hepatitis; his yellow skin was almost perfectly matched by the only nice pajamas he had, a bright yellow pair. Since he was a captive audience in bed, we dressed dolls and swept into his room, where he was to judge the fairest. We redressed them again and again. I can't remember if we ran out of doll clothes or he ran out of patience.

After Mother died, I think Daddy felt the burden of all the parenting fall heavily upon him. He made an extra effort to do what he could to fulfill Mother's nurturing role (such as writing to all of us kids once a week while we were at school). Once I had an assignment to speak about someone who had been a mother role model; I chose my father. At the same time, we grew up with the feeling that big, strong Daddy was taking care of us. My sister Gwen said she remembers our mother telling her this: "My love for your father was strong when we were married, but it grows stronger with each passing year of our marriage." Looking back, our home was as it should have been—fun and safe as a solid rock.

Jackie adds:

After my mother died, I experienced a tenderness in my father that I hadn't known before. When home from boarding school, it was just the two of us. Finding myself the "woman of the house" at thirteen, I dutifully poured over recipe books. Often the results were less than savory. My father ate whatever was prepared, making no distinction between gourmet and disaster. Later on, adjusting to college and navigating through life in a new country (America) proved to be difficult for me. When I penned my struggles to Daddy, his responses were always thought out and meaningful. He offered to fly home. Even though I declined the offer, as a daughter I felt cherished and tenderly cared for.

I only remember Daddy crying once when I was young. He cried silent tears when he was listening to the reel-to-reel tape of his father's funeral. After Mother and Jill died, all things sweet and sad brought on the tears. I was home from school for six weeks after my mother died. When we'd get up in the morning, Daddy would have been up for hours already. We'd find him in the living room with an open Bible on his knees, a praise tape playing, and tears streaming down his face. Praise is the way through heartache. My father never let bitterness steal away his joy.

My father's faith is true and unshakable. All the complexities of life are swallowed up into this: God is good and loves him.

*Terrie Foulkes Caisley,*
*Jackie Foulkes Royster,*
*and Gwen Foulkes Amborski*

One hazy afternoon on a tennis court in the heart of Bluegrass country (Lexington, Kentucky), I first met Jim. I stared across the net at this silver-maned lion, surprised at what an excellent player he was. When I occasionally got a shot by his speedy reflexes, the good doctor would respond with a resounding "great day!" It was an unusual colloquialism in Lexington, and it was not the last time Dr. Foulkes, on furlough from Mukinge, Zambia, surprised me.

In 1988, I was blessed to spend nearly a month in South Central Africa. A good portion of that time passed under the roof of Jim and Martha Foulkes's home, enjoying their warm hospitality. I was mesmerized by missionary stories shared around the dinner table and on hospital rounds. Unbeknownst to either Jim or me, the seeds for this book were planted on that trip, and some fifteen years later God has watered those seeds and brought forth this fruit.

"Did you hear Jim's tale about . . . ?" was a common response that I heard when I first met Jim's family and friends. "Picture being lost in the bush, the weather sweltering in triple digits," one would say. "With his tongue swollen so dry that he could not spit, Jim raised the point of his rifle at a distant wildebeest and pulled the trigger. Possible death by dehydration was staved off, as the doctor and the game guard with him drank down the milk from the wildebeest's mammary glands."

"The taste? Just wonderful," said Jim.

". . . An enraged hippo stormed out of the river and charged Jim, who had his gun slung low at his waist, with no time to get it snugged tightly onto his shoulder. Jim squeezed the trigger in the nick of time, stopping two tons of hippo in its tracks while nearly pulling Jim's arms out of their sockets in the process. He was lucky to wield a scalpel thereafter, the soreness not leaving his arms for several weeks."

"Had Foulkes not become a missionary, he would have been a test pilot or an astronaut," mused college friend Jim Adams. Zambia was still Northern Rhodesia (Northern Rhodesia became Zambia in a peaceful handover from England in 1964) when Jim arrived there, so he witnessed firsthand the creation of a new nation and lived through the convulsions of statehood, once even entertaining President Kenneth Kaunda in his home.

Walking through the wild landscape of the bush near Mukinge brought many of these stories to life. There was the time Jim and a hunting buddy were nearly overcome with dehydration, far from any potable water. They drank from a pond that four hundred buffalo had been in the night before; that gave a new twist to half and half—it was as much urine as it was water. They survived, even if their bellies were a bit queasy.

It was part of the job description for a doctor at Mukinge to kill one elephant annually for the hospital patients to eat. (The meat was either dried or frozen for later use.) An animal was dispatched, and the hunting party had a long way to go to retrieve the vehicle in which to transport the meat. Jim agreed to wait with the elephant to fend off any interloping animals. It was in the wee hours of the morning, with hyenas on the prowl, when the hunting party reached Jim again, concerned for his safety. With nocturnal Africa surrounding him, Jim had leaned himself against a tree and was sleeping peacefully.

"Working in the bush was often very tiresome," a friend said. "Jim once fell asleep during a lecture—while giving it!" Doctor Wenninger, Jim's fellow colleague, remembers Jim being hard to faze. Wenninger was summoned by Jim's frantic wife, Marilynn, when she found Jim unconscious on their bathroom floor, his face a bloody mess after a motorcycle wreck. "Oh, he's dead!" cried Marilynn. Wenninger examined Jim, then unceremoniously slapped his face (the uninjured side). Jim's eyes popped open and he snapped, "Hey doc, what's up?"

In 1998, Dr. Foulkes was feted by the World Medical Mission, when Franklin Graham presented him the prestigious Award for Excellence in Medical Missions. Then in 2000, Jim received the Alumni Achievement Award from the Ohio State University College of Medicine and Public Health. In 2002, Jim was honored by the Lima (Ohio) City Schools when he was inducted into the Distinguished Alumni Hall of Fame. No one who knew Jim was too surprised, "Dr. Foulkes obviously had the devotion of his staff and patients," said Marjorie Harstine, a missionary nurse who worked with Jim for more than thirty years.

God's calling on Jim's life was to heal with steel—by the sword of the Word and by a surgeon's scalpel. I helped Jim write this book because I wanted people to walk a little way down the road of life on which the Lord had sent James Raymond Foulkes.

*Joe Lacy*

to africa
with love

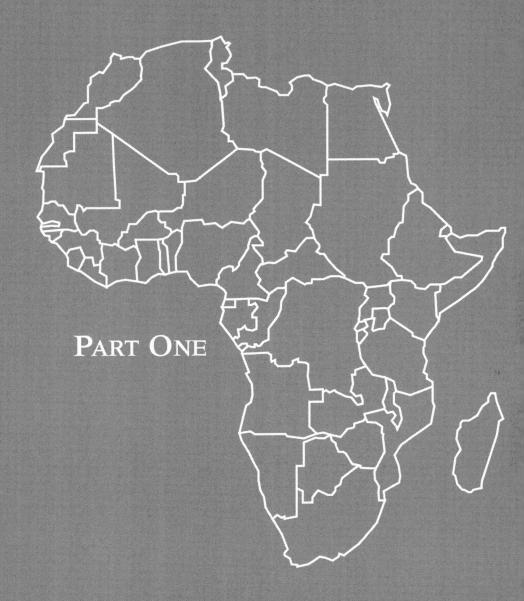

PART ONE

# ChapterOne
## Wafwa—A Poor Start

H e had only learned a few words in Kikaonde during his first three months among the Bakaonde tribe in Northern Rhodesia (later Zambia) but he knew what *Wafwa* meant— She's dead!

He also felt that he might be driving to his own death. He had been warned that in the eye-for-an-eye, life-for-a-life culture of the Bakaonde tribe, he could be speared to death by the dead girl's relatives. Usually, the relatives track down the murderer who has fled deep into the bush for his life.

He could see the body of the teenage girl wrapped in a hospital sheet in the rear mirror, her head resting on the lap of her wailing mother. *When is she going to stop screaming?* he wondered. Every time his station wagon hit a bump on the rough African road, it seemed to make the woman sob even louder.

But James R. Foulkes, a freshly-arrived medical missionary from Ohio, knew he was no murderer. The seventeen-year-old patient had died on the operating table. It had been an accident, but Jim still felt responsible. And he was determined to deliver the body to the family and suffer the consequences despite the danger involved.

*If I die, I die*, he told himself.

Fleeting thoughts of his wife and young children back at the mission station ran through his fevered mind. He pushed them aside, replacing them with thoughts of how the tragedy had unfolded.

The teenager had walked ten miles with her mother to the mission hospital with a common complaint. She had been married a year and she still was not pregnant; her impatient husband was threatening divorce. In that masculine dominant culture, little thought is given to the possibility that the man could be the infertile one; he may have even sterilized her by giving her an

*Map of Africa.*

unwanted nuptial gift of gonorrhea that could have scarred shut her fallopian tubes.

The method used at Mukinge to correct that most prevalent cause of infertility was a tubal insufflation (TI) procedure by which air is hand-pumped into the woman's uterus through the cervix in an effort to blow open any part of the fallopian tubes scarred down by infection.

The young doctor had been taught how to do a TI by his mentor, Dr. Bob Foster, a veteran bush doc and founder of Mukinge Hospital. They used the old tried-and-true formula of the under-doctored Third World—"see one, do one, teach one." Jim had already performed forty to fifty of the much-in-demand procedure in the few weeks before this particular girl showed up at the hospital.

Mukinge Hospital's reputation as an infertility clinic had spread rapidly after Dr. Foster had used the TI procedure to cure the barren wife of the paramount chief of the Bakaonde tribe five years earlier. The success of that procedure scored a medical breakthrough. It helped wean the local population from their total dependence on *ñangas* (witch doctors) and their herbal concoctions. It became obvious that the mission doctors' magic was more potent than that of the local practitioners. The big belly of the pregnant senior wife sent shivers down the backs of witch doctors wherever she appeared. Western missionary medicine had dealt ignorance and superstition a blow. The mission hospital had won instant recognition.

Now, however, bouncing along in the station wagon toward the dead girl's village, Jim was sure that he would be kicked out of the country by the Ministry of Health or rejected by the locals who would tag him as the young doctor who killed people. More than that, there was the possibility that his own life could be ended that day.

Jim had already experienced how violent Kaonde villagers could be when angry family members broke into the hospital one day with the intent of killing one of his patients. Their son/brother had been killed in a hunting accident. Jim's patient was his hunting partner who, though seriously wounded by the beast, had survived. To the family that could mean only one thing: the patient had killed their relative by conjuring up a magic leopard through the black magic of a ñanga.

After the dead man's angry family had stormed into the hospital, murderous revenge was eventually thwarted by a courageous orderly and a night watchman who alerted Jim. Staff members gathered to protect the frightened patient, while Jim took the leader of the clan to the police station four miles away. (When the case was tried in the chief's local court, Jim's patient was indeed found guilty of a witchcraft killing. He was ordered to give his muzzle loader to the grieving family for compensation.)

Jim kept slowly turning over in his mind how a routine, no-risk procedure, not requiring anesthesia or even an IV drip, could go so wrong. He reviewed how he had attempted to pump air through the young patient's left fallopian tube using a blood pressure bulb and metal insufflator. A gauge allowed him to see how much pressure was being pumped into the system. Too little pressure would not blow out the clogged tube, and too much could rupture it. A favorable sign of success is the sound of air bubbling into the abdomen, as heard through a stethoscope. In this case there was no sound. The right tube was the same story. Jim then withdrew the insufflator, disappointed, but not concerned. He decided not to tell the husband, since that would only make him divorce his wife even more quickly.

Lill Brannon, the veteran surgical nurse who was assisting Jim, suddenly called out, "Doctor, the patient's eyes are closed and she doesn't appear to be breathing!" That was followed, after a quick exam, by the shocker, "And she's not responsive!"

Jim quickly bent over the patient, searching for a carotid pulse, listening and looking for any evidence of air exchange. He could not hear or feel anything. Perhaps a large air bubble had entered into a vessel in her uterine wall and made its way centrally, causing a lethal air embolism.

Lill quickly placed an Ambu bag on the patient and pumped oxygen into her lungs while Jim compressed her chest to keep her heart pumping. After five minutes, she still had no heartbeat on her own. No external defibrillator was available in those early days. Jim then injected adrenaline directly into her heart muscle while both he and the nurse kept on with their CPR. The adrenaline had no effect.

In desperation, he opened her chest and started manual cardiac massage. With his gloved right hand around her heart, he was able to empty it by regular compression to make sure the blood was adequately perfusing the brain. Forty desperate and anguished minutes passed. Jim knew the patient was dead. But he kept up the charade, praying for a miracle. No miracle occurred. A young healthy woman had walked into the operating room only an hour ago and now she lay dead on the operating table. He had done nothing different from what he had done many times before. Doctor Foster had performed the procedure hundreds of times with not a single adverse effect.

Now it was Jim's sad duty to tell the teenager's mother that her daughter was dead. Sharing the bad news would be difficult in itself, but it was made even more difficult by the fact that he did not know enough Kikaonde to communicate without a translator. But the mother could easily see that the young doctor was visibly shaken and barely able to talk; she undoubtedly got the message even before Jim began to speak.

"Mama, I must tell you," Jim said, with tears in his eyes, "that we got into a big problem while we were trying to help your daughter. She stopped breathing and we then breathed for her and kept her heart beating for forty minutes, but after that long of a time we finally had to admit that we failed. I am so sorry to tell you that your daughter is dead."

The mother let out a blood-curdling shriek and fell to the floor, rolling around and screaming. Jim felt like joining her. But that was foreign to his culture, so he suffered in silence, helplessly watching the grief-stricken mother roll on the ground.

Dr. Foster warned Jim about the very real danger of taking the dead girl back to her village. It was an eye-for-an-eye culture. But Jim had made up his mind. He was too wracked with remorse to listen to reason. Recognizing that his advice was not making an impact, Dr. Foster alerted the staff to stop working and pray during the entire time Jim was gone. (Following the tragedy, the hospital used only carbon dioxide rather than room air when doing a TI. Carbon dioxide doesn't form a gas in the blood. No further problems ever arose.)

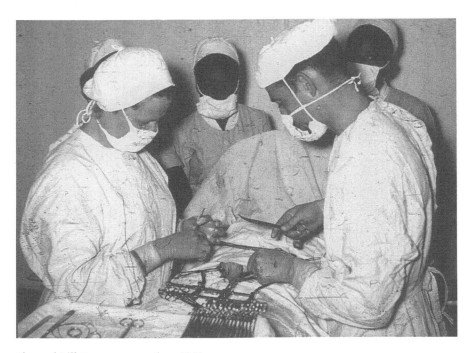

*Jim and Lill Brannon operating, 1960.*

After ten bumpy miles, Jim could see the village in the clearing. The mother, who had never stopped wailing once during the entire trip, became even louder the second they arrived at the village. She opened the door and fell to the ground, screaming, "Wafwa! Wafwa!" A small group of men, women, and children immediately gathered around the car.

Jim realized that what happened in the next second would determine his fate. If even one of the relatives started shouting in anger or picked up a rock or a spear, Jim would be killed. Perhaps the relatives saw his tears of sorrow or perhaps they were surprised at his willingness to face them. Perhaps, behind the scenes, the Father had commanded protective angels to come to his aid, since He had further work for Jim to do for the Kingdom.

Jim experienced the reality of Isaiah 59:19: "When the enemy shall come in like a flood, the spirit of the LORD shall lift up a standard against him."

Jim drove back to the mission station grateful to God for his deliverance but still fearful about the future. Would he lose his medical license? Would the people lose their confidence in him?

He had been told about a health inspector at a nearby district who had been playing doctor and, without any training, started doing unauthorized Caesarian sections. When one of his patients died, the ensuing investigation found him guilty and he was returned to England in disgrace. Jim wondered if that would happen to him!

It had been nine long years since he had first received his call to be a medical missionary. He had followed his dream through years of medical school, internship, residency, and support building. He was finally at the place of his calling, and it looked like it was all over before he could even get started!

But Jim knew that God never makes mistakes. He looked back on how God had revealed His will to him in a variety of ways. Tears again swelled up in his eyes as he looked back to the days of his youth when his mother prayed him to the mission field and his father encouraged him on the way in their home in Lima, Ohio. Jim had come a long way, but he wanted to go much further. He wanted to spend his life ministering to the medical and spiritual needs of the Kaonde tribe in Zambia.

"Please, God!"

Jim's thoughts once again turned homeward . . .

# ChapterTwo
## The Makings of a Missionary

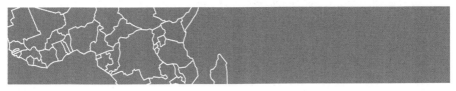

T he frustrated directors of the First National Bank of Lima, Ohio, were faced with a sensitive subject on their monthly agenda: How to get William R. "Billy" Foulkes, their executive vice president and senior trust officer, to stop parking his seven-year-old 1936 Dodge in front of the bank every day. The status-conscious directors felt their vice president's aging car detracted from the public image of both the man and the bank.

Jim recalled, "The directors didn't order Dad to get a new car but the fact that the topic even appeared embarrassed him. So he went out and bought one of the biggest cars he could find."

The new car was a 1940, twelve-cylinder, light blue Lincoln—a real gas guzzler, just when gas rationing was about to get underway. In addition to enhancing the bank's prestige, the high-powered auto also increased Jim's popularity. It made it a bit easier to get a date and the family cars of his buddies didn't have a chance when those twelve cylinders fired up in a drag race.

Jim was not an active Christian in high school. He sang in the church choir and was active in the youth fellowship and Boy Scouts, but he was not, however, considered especially religious by his classmates. (Years later, when Jim attended a twenty-fifth high school reunion and was asked, "What are you doing?", his answer that he was a missionary invariably brought a response similar to, "You're kidding!")

Although Jim came from a well-to-do family, the house in which his family lived was in a middle-class neighborhood. In fact, the Lima bank's junior executives lived in much larger homes than did their executive vice president's family.

The elder Foulkes's modest lifestyle stemmed from his growing up on a farm where high value was placed on every hard-earned dollar. Because Billy was needed full time on the farm, he had to wait to finish his education, plodding along little by little. After leaving the farm for the city, he enrolled in evening classes at Lima Business College. Billy's formal education finally culminated in a master's degree from Rutgers Graduate School of Banking when he was in his mid-forties.

His entrance into banking came when the president of the Lima Trust Bank (later the National Bank of Lima) went to the principal of the Lima Business College because he needed another teller. He asked, "Who is your best student?" That happened to be Billy Foulkes. The event made a lifetime banker out of him, and he spent his entire career on the corner of the town square at the big bank that his wife always called "Billy's bank." He rose rapidly in the ranks, becoming the bank's executive vice president and senior trust officer, a position Billy held until he was seventy years old.

But Billy Foulkes was no modern-day Scrooge interested only in counting money. He was a man of high morals with a strong religious streak. He joined the Trinity Methodist Church, where he served as chairman of the church's deacons and was the superintendent of the Sunday school. Billy's other good works included serving on the regional council of the Boy Scouts and being a founding officer of the Lima Chamber of Commerce and the Lima Convalescent Home.

Highly respected in the community and successful in his career, Billy Foulkes still felt something was lacking in his life . . .

That heart yearning would eventually be met through a feisty, vivacious instrument of God's grace named Ruth Beery. It was Ruth who would make the young banker realize that the almighty dollar could never take the place of Almighty God, and that salvation was all by grace, not by works.

Ruth Beery had enrolled at Moody Bible Institute in the early 1920s to further her knowledge of Scripture and to improve her singing voice, *not* to be told how to fix her hair. A crusty dean of women at Moody informed Ruth she would have to remove a hairpiece covering a near-bald spot or leave the institute. The spunky student didn't hesitate. She packed her bags, closed them defiantly, and walked out the door—her head held high and hairpiece firmly in place.

Oberlin College's Conservatory of Music was Ruth's next stop, where she spent a year polishing her gifts as a voice major. She then traveled as a soloist with an evangelistic team for almost a year after leaving Oberlin. Shortly after that, Ruth moved to Lima, where she secured a position with the Trinity Methodist Church as the parish visitor. A gregarious, friendly person, Ruth had never met a stranger. The Methodist pastor had chosen the right person to represent the church to the public.

Billy Foulkes was attending Trinity at the time and dating the church organist, Nell Kriete, Ruth's best friend. For whatever reason, the banker preferred the parish visitor to the organist. Surprisingly, the switch in girlfriends was made without anyone's feelings getting hurt, and Nell and Ruth remained lifelong friends.

"Aunt Nell was always very close to our family," Jim remembered. "She was our first piano teacher and a wonderful model for us. She never married and adopted our family and vice versa."

The Foulkes family attended Trinity for years. As a youngster, Jim was continuously mystified as to why the family always sat in the same pew up front when no one else ever sat in any of the first five rows. Whenever the church doors opened, that third pew would be filled with the Foulkes family.

One dramatic event in the life of Trinity Methodist Church was the arrival of Dr. E. Stanley Jones for a three-day preaching mission in 1939. "Our church was favored in hosting E. Stanley Jones," Jim recalled, "only because our pastor, J. Ira Jones, was a dear friend and classmate of his from the Asbury College class of '07." By that time, Dr. E. Stanley Jones was well known as the author of more than twenty books. "My mother was enough of a fan of his to have read all of them as soon as they were published," Jim said.

But as well as being a prominent author, Dr. Jones was well known for being an effective evangelist in India. His focus, however, was more on reaching the upper caste Indian leaders than the lower castes where most of the missionary effort was directed. The Christian Ashrams that he directed allowed the attendees to ask their questions and express their doubts in a retreat setting where he clearly presented the claims of Christ.

Mahatma Ghandi was seriously considering Christianity at one point and attended an Ashram that was directed by Dr. Jones.

*Jimmy and Dicky.*

Ghandi's final, sad conclusion was that he highly respected Christ and His teachings. He only had a problem with Christ's followers.

The challenge that was forcefully presented by Dr. E. Stanley Jones to "follow Christ" was reinforced by the Holy Spirit, and twelve-year-old Jim Foulkes wanted to be a sincere follower.

The evangelist was not making it easy, since he required that anyone responding to his invitation should come forward and kneel at the altar. As far as Jim knew, that altar was used exclusively as the place where you knelt to take communion. He had never seen it used as a place for a penitent sinner to come and beg for mercy, forgiveness, and cleansing. "I could hardly imagine walking down the carpeted, unfamiliar 'sawdust trail' in our austere church except that the Holy Spirit was drawing me more strongly than the fear of man was tempting me to stay cemented in my seat like every other person in the congregation," Jim commented.

Jim had no memory of his transaction with God as he knelt at the mourners' bench, but he was counseled by Dr. Jones. "The sincerity of my desire to follow Jesus was proven by the fact that for the next two years I prayed and read my Bible every day and was serious about being a disciple," Jim said.

The family was involved for years in what Jim described as a form of comfortable Christianity. Then God used Ruby Worthheimer, the widow of a converted Jewish rabbi, as an agent of change in the lives of Ruth and many other women from main-line churches who attended Ruby's Bible study at the YMCA.

Ruth gradually began to see that all of her church activities and good works could not save her. The Scripture as taught by Mrs. Worthheimer was clear: "For by grace are ye saved by faith, and that not of yourselves, it is the gift of God, not of works, lest any man should boast" (Eph. 2:8–9). Ruth saw herself as a lost sinner and turned to her Savior to become a new creation in Christ. Comfortable Christianity was out, New Testament Christianity, in all of its pristine purity and power, was in. And the world began to change for the Foulkes family from that moment.

Ruth's enthusiasm over her new relationship with Christ proved infectious. Within the year following her conversion, her husband became a true believer. Ruth was determined that Billy would be grounded in the Bible; she faithfully read a passage of Scripture every day so that by the end of the year they had covered the entire Bible. On some mornings she would even follow her husband into the bathroom, reading the day's assignment while he shaved! She then trailed him out of the bathroom to the breakfast table, still reading while he ate his breakfast.

Ruth Foulkes made her dining room a center of Christian fellowship and Bible teaching. Every week following Mrs. Worthheimer's morning Bible class, Ruth invited the teacher and eight or ten of the women to her home for a meal. This gave the ladies an opportunity to receive more in-depth answers to their questions while breaking bread with their instructor. It was a time of growth and sharing for all.

Ruth's mentoring at meals sparked a flame of love for the Bible in the heart of her husband. Billy joined the Gideons, a national organization dedicated to placing Bibles in hotel and motel rooms around the world. Billy's leadership qualities resulted in his being named to both state and local offices in the organization. He was enthusiastic about helping the local Gideon camp place Bibles in every hotel and motel in the area around Lima. During World War II, he also helped to get a pocket-sized New Testament and Psalms book into the hands of every young man inducted into the military in the local county. (Jim would get his when he boarded a troop train in mid–1945.)

Jim's father set an example that his son always admired. During World War II, gasoline was rationed. The government issued stamps to car owners with which to buy limited amounts of fuel (the phrase "fill 'er up" went out of vogue in WWII). Being scrupulously honest, Billy would turn in his unused stamps at the end of each month—much to the astonishment of the official who issued them.

"I respected my father greatly, even though at the time I was buying gas ration 'C' stamps on the black market when Dad gave me the car keys on the weekend. I was weak. Yet I knew that someday I wanted to be just like my father—straight as an arrow," Jim said.

During his high school days, Jim seemed to live in two different worlds. He loved to tool around town in his father's Lincoln, going to the same places that other teenagers did. He bluntly admitted that he cheated on tests and "did other things that I knew were wrong."

But at home, Jim was thrilled to hear exciting stories of pioneer missionaries going to foreign lands where the name of Jesus had never been uttered. Many had even given their lives for the sake of the gospel, such as John and Betty Stam who were martyred in China shortly after graduating from Moody Bible Institute.

The stories were told by Miriam Bracken, a representative of Gospel Recordings and an intimate friend of Ruth Foulkes. Miriam spent a great deal of time in their home. "Even though I wasn't a committed Christian early on when she made our home hers, Miriam's influence in my spiritual life was second only to my mother's," Jim recalled. Miriam had made the acquaintance of those in leadership positions in faith missions, many of whom she directed to the Foulkes home. (Hospitality was one of Ruth's great gifts.)

It was not by chance that among those who enjoyed the hospitality of the Foulkes home were Ken Strachen, director of the Latin American Mission (LAM), and Ezra Shank, the director of the South Africa General Mission (SAGM). Jim would one day go to Zambia with SAGM (later called the Africa Evangelical Fellowship [AEF], and later still wedded with SIM). His older brother, Dick, went to Costa Rica to serve with the LAM.

Whatever Jim's spiritual status, his mother had committed both of her sons to missionary service long before they had committed themselves fully to Christ. Mother Foulkes admonished her boys that if the Lord has called one to become a missionary, then one should not stoop to becoming the president of the United States.

# The Makings of a Missionary

Jim had no ambitions of being president, and it made him uncomfortable when his mother would tell his school chums that she hoped that both of her sons would be called to the mission field. (Mother Foulkes often nudged God through prayer to make that call loud and clear . . . and soon!)

Both of Jim's parents placed a premium on excellence in all areas of life. They espoused the biblical dictum of "Whatever your right hand finds to do, do it with all your might" (Eccl. 9:10 NIV). Achieving excellence, however, came easier to the musically talented and intellectually gifted older brother, Dick, than it did to Jim. Dick consistently scored the highest among the college prep students in Lima Central High School and became the only Ohio pianist to be accepted by the prestigious Juilliard Conservatory of Music in 1946.

The less studious and younger missionary-to-be emphasized social life above academics. Jim's dark good looks and pleasant personality made him popular with the coeds in both high school and college. Athletics was his forte, not classroom exercises.

Jim often ran the mile-and-a-half from school to home, which eventually paid unexpected dividends. During his high school freshman year, track coach, Ron Dotson, had all the boys run around the block. Jim easily led the pack, impressing the coach. He said, "Jimmy, I'm going to make you the best half miler in the state."

Jim quickly saw that excelling in sports was a way to distinguish himself. The fuel shortage caused by the war had eliminated all high school competitive sports except football, basketball, and track. That denied Jim the other three sports at which he excelled— tennis, swimming, and cross country—leaving track as his only option. He vowed that he would fulfill his coach's promise and become Ohio's best half miler.

Strenuous training under the watchful eye of Coach Dotson paid off in his senior year. At the district finals, Jim won the half-mile run, with the third best time in the state.

Buoyed by this victory, Jim believed he had a good shot at winning the state finals. But it was not to be. He could never close the distance between himself and the lead pack of five runners. And for good reason! The winner had sliced three seconds off the state record, having run exactly as fast as the college senior who won the half mile at the national collegiate championships the same day.

"My timing was off. That was not the day to be competing against a seventeen-year-old boy who already was a world-class half miler," Jim joked.

Jim may not have won the state title, but he still won plaudits in the local newspaper for being the only track man from Lima to qualify for the state finals. (Jim had to wait a long time to be a state champion. At the North Carolina senior games in 2003, he set a new state record for the 5,000 meters in his age category.)

"The write-up on the sports page helped boost my already reasonably developed self-esteem a few notches beyond what was healthy," Jim recalled. "It gave me a partial answer to the question asked by every teenager, *Who am I?*"

Though proud of her son's achievement, all this was irrelevant to the little lady from Lima beseeching God to make her son a missionary. Ruth's mind was more on the words of the prophet Isaiah than on the local sports page: "How beautiful on the mountains are the *feet* of those who bring good news, who proclaim peace, who bring good tidings, who proclaim salvation . . ."(Isa. 52:7 NIV, author's emphasis).

"In guiding me toward my life's calling, no one had more influence than my mother. I learned how to pray from her, and to this day I still pray as she did. I have always been sobered by the knowledge that to whom much has been given, much will be required. I was given a great storehouse of valuable gifts by my godly mother," Jim said earnestly.

The devout prayer warrior never doubted that God was guiding her younger son toward the mission field, whatever his short-term decisions. But Jim had his mind on other matters. He was looking for a college with a good track team.

# ChapterThree
## Off to the Army and Asbury

Wheaton College in suburban Chicago has long had an outstanding reputation as one of the finest academic Christian colleges in the country. But in 1945, it was the Flying Parson, Gill Dodds, the college's famous track coach, who attracted Jim more than the college's academic standing.

For a number of years, Dodds held the indoor world record for the mile. Jim had witnessed Dodds's running one of his marvelously orchestrated races at the Cleveland Relays. As a Christian, Dodds felt it was wrong to try to beat his opponents, so he ran only against the clock. At each quarter mile, his trainer would call out the time.

"By the half-mile mark, Dodds had won a clear lead (in Cleveland) since no one else could run as fast as he did indoors," Jim remembered. "I had respect for Gill's strong Christian stand, but more important, I had placed him on a pedestal since he was the best."

Jim applied for admission to Wheaton, mentioning that he was interested in the track team as a half miler. But he didn't have much hope of being admitted because of his poor high school grades. Much to his surprise, the college fired back a telegram wanting to know how fast he could run the half mile. He was even more surprised when he was actually accepted for the fall term.

But once again Jim's plans did not jibe with God's plans for his life. He received his high school diploma in June of 1945, and his draft notice in August, just a few weeks after the dropping of the atomic bomb on Hiroshima on August 9. College was placed on hold.

Many years later, Jim was at the museum in Los Alamos, New Mexico, where replicas of the bombs dropped on Nagasaki and Hiroshima are displayed. There was a chorus of "wasn't that awful" from bystanders. He kept his mouth shut, agreeing that it *was* awful, but at the same time realizing that without those bombs, his bones would likely be lying bleached alongside those of countless other Americans on some South Pacific island.

It was fortunate for Jim that the war was over shortly before he was inducted; but like many of his age who entered the military as a teenage boy, he emerged from the service a mature young man. Much of that maturing took place during his one-year tour of duty in Panama.

God kept His hand on Jim in the military. A sergeant major in the Army invited Jim to attend a Navigator's Bible study in the home of an employee of the Canal Zone. The meeting always began with testimony time with a number of GIs telling how the Lord had directed them in some specific way during the week. The testimonies had the ring of truth in them and deeply impressed Jim. But it was the weekly Bible study where the teacher made plain the plan of salvation from the Word that the gospel gradually began to penetrate his stony heart.

Jim thought back to the commitment to Christ that he had made at the altar of the Trinity Methodist Church as a twelve-year-old boy. That was a sincere promise to follow Jesus and had a significant impact on his life, but it had lacked the theological content that Jim now needed as an eighteen-year-old. Since the old commitment had faded considerably in high school, it was time to be reaffirmed as a fresh covenant with a more complete understanding of the process of being reconciled to God. Jim testified:

> I accepted the good news that Christ had carried my sins with Him on the cross. Repenting of my sins and leaving them at the foot of the cross, allowing Christ to be my Savior and my Lord, was an event that radically changed my life.

> I experienced the truth of 1 Corinthians 5:17, that old things had passed away and all things had become new. I had enlisted in the King's army for life. There was no turning back.

The Navigators had rules that Christian soldiers were expected to obey. One was "No Bible, no breakfast." An additional rule was to pray down the day at night on one's knees, as well as to say hello to God in the morning. It was while on his knees by his cot in the open barracks that Jim experienced his first form of harassment as a Christian, a not-too-gentle kick in the ribs from a fellow GI. Some of the others made sarcastic remarks about Foulkes getting religion; but Jim's sincerity and commitment eventually made an impression on his hedonistic buddies.

"Having to take a public stand for my new faith in the face of ridicule was the best training I could have hoped for," Jim recalled, looking back on his military experience. "It cemented my resolve for the rest of my life, to never be ashamed of Jesus."

Following the Navigator's system, Jim memorized Scripture daily, changing his spiritual diet from milk to meat. Navigators made memorizing Scripture easy by giving each GI a small packet filled with Bible verses printed on business-size cards. A GI could pull a verse from his packet while standing in the chow line or waiting for a roll call and have plenty of time to commit the verse to memory.

Those twelve months spent at Fort Clayton along the Panama Canal were a time of spiritual growth and joy for the young believer. Each week following Sunday school and church services, several GIs in the Navigator group would eat together at the PX and then return to the empty church to spend the afternoon sharing the blessings and trials of the week. In contrast, they were surrounded the rest of the week by men interested mostly in wine, women, and carousing.

Jim explained, "I went into the army as a typical eighteen-year-old kid with no particular goal or sense of direction. I came out as a committed Christian with a strong desire to please and obey my new Master."

Jim was deeply moved by the deaths in the Battle of the Bulge of two of his friends from his high school track team. He said, "That had a great effect on me. If I had considered giving my life for my country, why couldn't I give my life for the Lord?"

Upon his return to Lima following his discharge, Jim reapplied to Wheaton College without even mentioning his track exploits. Wheaton's academic requirements were high. A graduating senior had to be in the top section of his class to even be considered or else pass a stiff entrance exam. Jim came up short in both cases and was refused admission to Wheaton.

"I had become a non-student the last two years in high school," he stated. "And I obviously didn't do well enough on the entrance exam to overcome my lousy high school grades."

But our Lord is a God of second chances. He knew Jim better than Jim knew himself. God had a missionary in the making, and He would finish the good work that He had begun.

In April of 1947, the Foulkes family took a vacation to Florida. Still shopping for a Christian liberal arts college for Jim, the family decided to make a stop on the way to visit Wesleyan-oriented Asbury College in Wilmore, a small town on the edge of the Bluegrass region of central Kentucky. The area is noted for its thoroughbred racehorse farms of rolling, green-pasture fields bordered by miles of white fences.

Although a small college of only seven hundred students in 1947, it had an expansive campus that was in full spring bloom when the Foulkeses visited. Jim and his family walked around the campus, admiring its beauty (enhanced by attractive coeds) and talking with students and faculty. Many of the students had come to Asbury to prepare for the ministry. Even though he didn't have a clear-cut call as so many of the other students did, he had made up his mind about one thing: he wanted to enroll at Asbury College.

"Everything looked perfect to me. It was love at first sight. That love affair didn't wear off for the whole four years," he fondly recalled. Jim at last had found an academic environment where he was comfortable as well as challenged.

Many of Asbury's male students had fought in World War II and were several years older and more mature than those fresh out of high school. Because of their age and military experience, the new college crop of veterans generally were more serious about their education and commitment to Christ than were the younger students. Jim explained:

> Several of my friends at Asbury had given their lives to the Lord while fighting on some South Pacific island. Asbury was just the right place for me, since I found some friends who were miles ahead of me in their journey with Jesus. I learned more from them than I did from some of my professors about taking up one's cross, denying oneself, and following Jesus. They were excellent role models.

The theology taught at Asbury had a Wesleyan emphasis of personal holiness, and worship was sometimes loud and emotional.

Students prayed out loud, whether praying alone in their closets or all seven hundred together during chapel. It took some time for Jim to get used to hearing occasional "amens" and "hallelujahs" voiced by the students and even some faculty during chapel. He had never witnessed anything like that at eleven o'clock Sunday morning in the third pew of Trinity Methodist Church in Lima. He found out that he liked a participatory worship service much better than mere pew warming.

John Wesley's theology included the practical as well as the spiritual. His handbook of *Methodist Discipline* that he gave to all of his circuit riders even included direction on how to feed and bed down their mounts at night, the better to be able to ride in the morning to tend to the souls of men. Asbury (named after the first American Methodist bishop, Francis Asbury) required students to spend their weekends in practical service. This meant that some students such as Jim's roommate, Gene Frazer, would drive hundreds of curvy miles every week to preach in rural churches in Kentucky and Ohio that had no resident pastors.

Some students stayed closer to home, going to nearby Lexington to pass out tracts or engage in open-air meetings on street corners. Jim felt more comfortable knocking on doors and witnessing to people privately than in the open air. Television had not permeated society in the 1940s, and Jehovah's Witnesses and Mormons had not yet immunized people against doorbell evangelists. "I was always amazed at how often people would open their doors and, sometimes, their hearts when we went calling," Jim remembered.

The longer he stayed at Asbury, the dream of becoming a medical missionary rather than a minister occupied his mind more and more. The science department was headed by Dr. Cecil Hamann, and Dr. Paul Ray was in charge of the chemistry section. "I found myself signing up for more and more science courses thanks largely to these two professors," he stated. "I highly respected the godly lives of these two men, as well as their brilliant minds."

Jim still considered himself a pre-theology major at this point. But his desire to take difficult science courses and to do well in them caused him to question whether or not he should change his major. He found in his second year that he could declare himself a pre-med major, but he still wasn't sure. One night he took a long walk down a moonlit back road outside of Wilmore. As he walked, he prayed, asking God to show him which path he should take: medical school or seminary. "No bright light flashed, but around 2:00 A.M. I felt strongly that I should at least apply to medical school," he said.

It was a turn toward a God-willed destination that he would follow all the way to Africa.

# ChapterFour
## The Holy Spirit Steps In

W hen Jim began applying to medical schools, he soon discovered that he faced a much greater challenge than he had in getting into college. His first-year college grades were below average; it wasn't until his second year that Jim's interest in academic subjects kicked in. But the scholastic damage had been done. He was the only pre-med candidate in his class to graduate without honors. There were ten applicants for every opening in medical school, most of whom were veterans who were serious students with excellent grades.

From all outward appearances, Jim's chances of getting into medical school were next to nil. But God sometimes uses the most unusual means—in this case, politics—His wonders to perform!

Perry Tanksley, a friend of Jim's, was running for student body president at Asbury. A shrewd strategist, Tanksley had the pre-theological vote sewn up. But he needed support from the science students to win, so he turned to Jim to round up the voters among the science electorate. Jim did; Perry won. And in the hallowed tradition of politics at any level, Jim was made Tanksley's vice president as a reward for his bringing in the political sheaves.

"That put me in *Who's Who in American Colleges and Universities,* oiling the hinges of the doors to medical school," Jim said, who still stands amazed at how God worked wonders in his life.

Jim applied to medical schools at Emory University in Atlanta and Ohio State University in Columbus. During personal interviews he was asked: "Why do you want to become a doctor?" Now Jim had an answer that he could give with conviction.

"I believe that I am called to be a medical missionary," he would reply. An embarrassed silence would follow this answer. Secular university admissions officials were not used to "God talk." It was acceptable for a student to say that he wanted to alleviate human suffering, for instance, but a student with a call from God only elicited suspicion.

So when the Ohio State College of Medicine sent Jim an acceptance letter, Jim regarded it as a gift from God. It further confirmed his strong belief that God was leading him to be a medical missionary *somewhere*. This belief was reinforced before leaving Asbury College, when Jim experienced two life-changing events that he would never forget.

The first took place at the InterVarsity Christian Fellowship missionary convention held in 1948 at the University of Illinois, Urbana. It was here that Jim came into contact with some twentieth-century heroes of missionary evangelism.

The second event would be in Wilmore, Kentucky, where the Holy Spirit would do a mighty work in what later became known as the Asbury Revival of 1950.

Jim Elliot, a senior at Wheaton College and president of the Student Foreign Missions Fellowship, was at the missionary conference. He had prayed that God would break in on the conference in Pentecostal power, causing hundreds of students to search their hearts to find out what God's plan was for their lives and then to act upon it.

"It was memorable to get to meet and talk with Jim Elliot at Urbana," Jim said. "We had several conversations at the conference, and later some correspondence, when I needed more information about the props."

With great interest, Jim had watched the skit that Elliot had written and directed, vividly showing the needs of the world. Jim was so impressed with the production that he wanted to copy it for use at an upcoming missionary conference at Asbury. Elliot gave Jim a copy of the script and even offered some suggestions on the backdrop props.

"With no thought that I was in touch with one of the missionary greats, I tossed his letter into a wastebasket after absorbing his advice," Jim said with obvious regret.

Jim Foulkes's defining moment at the Urbana convention came at the end. A tall, lean, flashily dressed young evangelist by the name of Billy Graham challenged the students to serve God on the mission field. Several hundred of the students—including Jim— signed the commitment card with the pledge: *"God being my helper, I commit myself to serving as a career foreign missionary."*

"That was my time of full and final commitment to a calling that I had been very interested in for a number of years," Jim said. "When I signed my name there was no turning back. The Lord asked 'Who will go?' and I answered, 'Here am I, send me.'"

Jim Elliot made the headlines when he was martyred on a sandy jungle beach in Ecuador along with four other young missionaries in 1956. If Elliot was anything, he was intense. He would not settle for half measures, having lived his life in accordance with the now oft-quoted words he penned: "He is no fool who gives away that which he can not keep to gain that which he can not lose."

Two Christian Jims left Urbana confirmed in their calling to serve God in the jungles, continents apart. One would die eight years later on an isolated beach with an Auca spear in his throat, slaughtered by the people he had come to serve. The other would serve the Lord a day at a time for thirty-eight years in an African bush hospital. Both fought the good fight and kept the faith. They will meet again on a new day.

If Jim's missionary call was confirmed at Urbana, he got a taste of what heaven must be like during the Wheaton-Asbury revivals early in 1950. Asked to describe the impact the Asbury revival made on him and others, Jim said:

Arrangements had been made for a friend and me to drive to Wheaton College for a long weekend in February 1950 to visit some of our friends. That was the very time a spontaneous revival had broken out on the Wheaton campus and classes had been cancelled for the week. On Saturday evening the student-led revival was in full swing, and when George Beverly Shea sang "Just As I Am," I felt a terrific tug from the Holy Spirit to go forward and make sure everything was clean. I poured out my heart to the Lord and confessed everything that the Spirit pointed out in my life that was displeasing to God. I knew that I was cleansed of all unrighteousness as John promises when one confesses one's sins.

When we returned to Asbury on Monday, our class was having a party when I felt an overwhelming conviction that I was supposed to share with them what was going on at Wheaton and what the Lord had done for me. A testimony was not on the agenda for the evening party, but I broke in and shared what I felt sure that I was supposed to leave with my classmates.

There were many other events on the campus being orchestrated by the Lord, like an all-night prayer meeting by some of the boys. On Thursday morning in chapel, February 23, 1950, a senior student by the name of Herb Vanvorce got up to confess what the Lord had just done for him, and at that moment the Holy Spirit swept into Hughes Auditorium. The Lord was high and lifted up and the train of His robe filled the chapel. As in Isaiah's day, the response of many to the Divine Presence was: "Woe unto me, for I am undone, and my eyes have seen the King, the Lord Almighty" (Isa. 6:5).

The large altar immediately began to fill up with students who were overcome with guilt over falling short of the mark. The tears of repentance were flowing. Then a pattern began to develop as the Holy Spirit took complete charge of the events. When students had made their peace with the Lord, they had a strong desire to share their victory with fellow students and a queue began to build up in front of the microphone.

The testimonies of victory were tremendously encouraging to all who heard, and the response from the audience was often a hymn of thanks to the Lord. It was a time of praise and worship since the Presence was almost palpable. Classes were suspended since nobody left the auditorium for the rest of the morning or the afternoon, and almost the entire student body remained in the chapel for the whole night.

The joy of being in the Divine Presence was so wonderful that the desire for food and sleep was completely overshadowed. I had no thought of leaving Hughes Auditorium for thirty-six hours. The water fountain and toilet in the basement sufficed. Classes were then suspended for the entire week. News of the revival was followed daily by the national media. People started flooding into Wilmore from far and wide, and included parents of students, but mostly just everyday followers of Jesus who were hungry and thirsty for righteousness. As the Lord promised in His beatitudes, they were filled. Not just filled, but filled to overflowing since one of the purposes of revival blessing is to pass it on.

In recalling the revival fifty years later, Jim asked and then answered the question: "Why did God choose to reveal Himself on the campuses of several Christian colleges all within one month?"

"They were spontaneous revivals," he commented. "The timing was God's, and there was no association with special speakers or prearranged meetings."

The revival fires spread from Wilmore across the southeastern section of the country, the geographical area from whence Asbury draws many of its students. Student groups spoke at dozens of churches, carrying the revival contagion with them. Jim was a member of the Men's Glee Club that was used by God to spread the revival fires. He explained how the group spread the flames:

It was a special privilege to be a member of the Men's Glee Club which had a heavy schedule of singing and ministering at churches, colleges and high schools during the spring break of 1950.

One vivid memory was ministering on a Sunday morning at a large church with a big group of university students present. We had just gotten into the second section of our concert program when the Holy Spirit brought a deep sense of conviction upon the congregation. University students and older members started flooding the altar. They were broken over the revealed enormity of their sins and there were tears of sorrow flowing from most of the penitents at the altar.

The amazing thing to us was that no testimony had yet been shared and no challenge yet given (that was still fifteen minutes away in our program). Even so, the Convicter of men's hearts came down in His own timing and interrupted our concert. We went down to assist the seekers who numbered more than one hundred.

As sins were confessed and abandoned, they were replaced by the joy of forgiveness and victory. The flame of revival fell upon every church and school we visited, and we rarely left an evening service before 2:00 A.M.

The refining fire that was kindled by a visit from a student group would often go on for weeks and months and spread to other churches and other towns . . . How great is our awesome Father. It was no surprise that a large number of our graduating class went into full-time Christian service.

In many ways the Wheaton-Asbury revivals mirrored the Great Awakening of the 1740s, which forever changed the spiritual contours of our nation. The preachers of the Awakening wanted people to know that outward morality was not enough for salvation. An inward change was necessary. An individual needed to deeply feel sin and unworthiness before a righteous God.

It would seem that the spiritual ingredients of any heart-felt, life-changing revival are the same whether in 1740 in New England or 1950 in Midwestern America. And why not? Is God not the same yesterday, today, and forever?

# ChapterFive
# Med School

J im got off to a stumbling start as a graduate student in medicine on the huge Ohio State University campus in Columbus when his grades hit rock bottom in the first quarter. The green med student's precarious academic standing had nothing to do with the fact that he had just transferred from a Christian liberal arts college of seven hundred students in Wilmore, Kentucky, to a state university of forty thousand students in metropolitan Columbus.

No, his problem stemmed from thinking that he would be doing the right thing by singing rather than studying for his first mid-term exam; so Jim left campus for the weekend to lead the singing at the statewide InterVarsity Christian Fellowship (IVCF) conference rather than hitting the books.

"I mistakenly thought the Lord would honor me for my interpretation of putting Him first," Jim recalled. "Even when I got home on Sunday evening, I didn't study since none of the Christians in our class studied on the Lord's day."

The first mid-term in anatomy was the next morning. Jim flunked it cold. The chances of bringing that failing grade up twenty points in the next two exams appeared impossible.

Even by buckling down and studying late into the night, Jim still only scored the class average of seventy-five on the next anatomy exam. That score only boosted his failing grade by five points. Jim then had to face that he might have to drop out of medical school. The first year medical class had been told that the lowest fifteen students would be dismissed at the end of the year. That dire possibility affected his entire being—body, mind, and soul. Going to sleep was now a struggle, and he began losing weight.

But Jim's biggest struggle was spiritual. He had been so sure that God had called him to go to medical school. Now he wasn't so sure. One night, unable to sleep, he got up, dressed, and went for a walk.

It all seemed so hopeless. Alone in the night, he wept and poured out his heart to the Lord.

Everyone knows a good cry can bring release and relief. Jim also felt a sense of comfort coming down from God. That divine peace that passes understanding enabled him to go back home and slip into a deep sleep that his exhausted body and troubled mind needed so badly.

"I'm sure that without the loving arms of the Lord around me, I would have gone under," Jim said.

Sometimes the Lord uses the arms of friends and family to do the embracing. Before beginning medical school in the fall of 1951, Jim had a visit in Lima from a young man who was a brother in the Lord and later would become Jim's best friend at OSU. Jim Diller only lived a few miles away. Their parents had met through the work of the Gideons. The two Jims had so much in common that they quickly bonded. Both were missionary candidates and would be going to OSU as classmates. Both were also good singers. Diller sang with the college quartet at Wheaton, where he also had been the captain of the track team.

The two prayed together and covenanted they would help each other stay true to their holy calling. They also discussed starting a Christian Medical Society chapter at OSU. With the aid of other students committed to missionary service—Bob Chapman, Hugh Frazer, and Dan Reynolds—they formed a chapter. The two buddies from Lima also teamed up with Frazer and Reynolds to form a quartet that was invited to sing at various churches in Columbus.

Diller, an honor student, stood by Jim when he was going through his trials at OSU. When Jim voiced doubts about making it through medical school, Diller would hear him out and then gently ask, "Who are you trusting in, Jim?" That question would always drive Jim back to the God of all comfort.

At one point, however, Jim felt the need to be with those who knew him best and loved him most, his parents. He called home. Dad and Mother Foulkes drove to Columbus to encourage and pray with their distraught son. Jim never forgot that visit. More than forty years later he would say, "They left me with peace. It was just like a visit with Jesus." God has many arms with which to hug His children.

*Four Ohio State med school buddies who all went to Africa after further training. From left to right: Dan Reynolds, '56 (Ethiopia); Jim Diller, '55 (Congo); Hugh Frazer, '56 (Angola); and Jim. The young men formed a quartet and sang and spoke in Columbus churches. Bob Chapman, '55, went to Ethiopia but was not in the quartet.*

When time for the dreaded anatomy final exam rolled around, Jim was primed, pumped, and ready. He found that he could shut his eyes and visualize every detail of the nerves and muscles he would have to identify. He knew that his greatest enemy was fear. But the Lord calmed Jim's nerves and he entered the exam room with an assurance that all would be well.

The final practical exam in anatomy required the students to follow each other around huge dissecting tables where nerves and muscles to be named were tagged on twenty cadavers. Every three minutes a bell would ring and every student had to move on to the next specimen. Jim recalls being in line behind a devout Catholic friend who kept one hand in his pocket counting his rosary as he moved from cadaver to cadaver. (Jim confined himself to a silent *Thank you, Lord,* when each glance at a nerve or muscle brought instant recognition.)

"Those body parts were old friends that I had been well acquainted with for many weeks," he said with a chuckle. The practical exam was followed by a written exam. The Lord gave Jim a clear head and a hand that wasn't shaking with fear. He left the room, his heart overflowing with praise.

Jim had aced the exams; he made an A. The A could have stood for "awesome;" it meant that he would pass the course. Jim didn't have any trouble passing his other subjects.

Jim remains convinced that the Lord intervened and corrected a bad mistake that he had made in not setting his priorities properly. "From that point on, no one could have convinced me that I was not born to be a medical missionary," he said. "Practicing medicine in America rather than Africa would have been a big problem for me."

Ironically, Jim almost repeated the same mistake in his second year. Once again the problem had to do with making a choice on how to properly divide his time between medicine and ministry.

OSU had a vibrant IVCF chapter with sixty or seventy students who met every Friday evening to hear a special speaker. Several of the members conducted Bible studies in their fraternity or sorority houses and in dormitories. When it came time to elect officers for the 1953–54 school year, Jim's name came up for president.

Jim was the only one in the chapter who had ever attended an IVCF camp that prepared students for leadership. In 1949, while still in Asbury, he had spent a month at Campus-in-the-Woods in Ontario, Canada, on the beautiful Lake of Bays. The experience had left an indelible impact. At the urgent and repeated request of the IVCF regional representative, Jim finally agreed to take the post of president with one caveat—the vice president would do most of the grunt work.

Jim soon discovered, however, that as president he still had to select the special speakers and write to them confirming dates and their accommodations. He also had to make sure that the speakers had the ability to communicate with college students.

Jim recalled meeting a special speaker, Joe Bayly, at the train station and entertaining him at his fraternity house. Bayly was the brilliant editor of *His Magazine*, the IVCF periodical that ran articles of practical help for Christian students studying at secular universities.

"Getting to spend so much time with this godly man is a memory that I treasure," Jim said. Bayly would minister to Jim on a much deeper level farther down the road. Bayly, who lost three of his children, wrote a moving booklet entitled "A View from a

Hearse" (Elgin, Ill.: David C. Cook, 1969). Jim would drink deeply from that little book to assuage his own grief years later.

It gradually became obvious to Jim that fulfilling his duties as president was taking too much of the time needed for studying. His grades had begun to slip. It was a difficult decision, but he resigned the office and handed the leadership over to his trusted friend, Jim Adams.

Out of his IVCF experience in both his first and second year in medical school, Jim came up with a principal on priorities that a Christian student with a long-range goal would do well to heed: "When trying to decide between opportunities for short-term ministry and the requirements for the long haul, never let the immediate overrule the distant future."

Despite his flirtation with disaster from over-commitment, Jim still relished the rich fellowship he found in IVCF and with fellow students in the Christian Medical Society.

"Overall, my experience in IVCF was of great value in preparing for God's service overseas," he said. It seems that God really doesn't let any of His obedient children waste any of their time. Everything still works to the good for those who love Him.

# Chapter**Six**
## Love and Marriage

J im was convinced that the Lord would provide him with a Christian wife as a helpmate on the mission field. And that conviction also put him in the valley of decision. He knew that he had to be selective in his dating, or he could fall in love with a Christian woman who had no interest in serving overseas. Jim had seen other missionary candidates stray from their calling by marrying women who did not share their vision. He was determined by God's grace never to get caught in that trap.

Asbury College seemed to be the ideal place to find a wife as many of the coeds on the campus believed they were called to missionary service. In his senior year, Jim dated art teacher Millie White, whom he admitted "was further down the road in her walk with Christ than I was."

Through that special relationship, Jim discovered that even dating had a spiritual dimension. Millie insisted that they always spend some time in prayer while on a date. She taught Jim a lesson in romance that he took with him from Asbury to graduate school.

"Millie introduced me to C. S. Lewis and Andrew Murray, two Christian writers who have remained heroes and mentors to me," Jim said.

While attending medical school in Columbus, Jim made a return visit to Asbury, where he met a Southern beauty who could have been a stand-in for Elizabeth Taylor. Needless to say, the Southern belle from Mississippi caught the eye of the Yankee from Ohio. The young lady had become a Christian as an aftermath of the Asbury revival. Several Asbury students from her church came back home for a weekend, triggering a mini-revival with their testimonies, and she immediately quit her job and headed off to Asbury herself. She quickly became what Jim later would call a rather serious acquaintance.

However, the girl he would later propose to was still being prepared by God for that important event.

Marilynn Hall, a pert, attractive brunette nursing student, entered Jim's life during his third year of medical school. Jim often led the singing at the Friday night IVCF meeting on campus. Marilynn, a superb pianist, attended the meetings sporadically. But when she did show up, she was always asked to play for the song service. Marilynn later would reveal that she only attended the IVCF meetings so she could write to her father and tell him she had gone.

Marilynn was much more faithful to her sorority than to IVCF. She had been selected to join the prestigious Alpha Omega Alpha (AOA) chapter that only accepted students who had been named to the National Honor Society in high school. She received an additional honor when she was picked from a large group of contestants to be the accompanist for the OSU Men's Glee Club. That meant that Marilynn was literally surrounded by twenty-one young men who only had to stop by the piano to ask for a date.

Marilynn was a freshman in the nursing program when Jim was a third-year med student. He also was seven years older than Marilynn. Jim erroneously assumed that his seniority would place him at the head of the line of boys seeking some quality time with their popular pianist. He was wrong. He would have to take a number and wait his turn the same as the singers. Unaccustomed to being treated so casually by a girl, Jim decided if he couldn't be number one or even number two, he would bow out. After all, he was still number one with the Southern belle in Mississippi.

But God would change both Jim's and Marilynn's plans.

It happened during Marilynn's second year in nursing. She was asked to play at a statewide InterVarsity conference. C. Stacy Woods, the IVCF general director and a transplant from Australia, was the speaker. The message struck home in Marilynn's heart. The Holy Spirit showed the talented pianist that she could not play at being a Christian. She could not inherit her father's faith.

Before leaving the conference, she confessed her sins and committed her life to Christ. She could now say without hesitation, "I *know* whom I have believed." She could no longer go to an IVCF meeting just to please her earthly father. Instead, she went because she enjoyed being in the company of other believers which was pleasing to her heavenly Father. To seal it, Marilynn consulted with her pastor and then underwent believer's baptism. She was a new creature in Christ.

Her new life gave Jim renewed hope. They both knew that they shared more than a love for music. The Son of God was their center, and both had a strong desire to serve Him.

"I was amazed at the deep thoughts and beautiful poetry that came out of her sanctified mind," Jim remembered years later, a little misty-eyed. "After only two evenings with the new Marilynn Hall I realized that I was in love with her."

But he wasn't sure she felt the same way about him. He would pretend his interest was only platonic while all the time believing that Marilynn could tell by the look in his eyes that he was hopelessly in love with her. But if she did, she never let on. It would take a bolt of lightning and a most inappropriate comment by Mother Foulkes to make them both remove their masks and reveal their true feelings.

A strong swimmer, Jim took Marilynn on a date to a water-filled stone quarry. Suddenly a storm rolled in very close to where they were swimming. Trapped by the electrical storm, they were in shallow water when a sharp crack of lightning struck close, sending Marilynn flying into Jim's arms. Jim always believed Marilynn's reaction was perhaps a preview "showing her that my arms would always be there to protect her and love her."

But Jim still was not sure he had completely won Marilynn's heart. He saw his brother as a trump card. He had long bragged about Dick's brilliance as a pianist to Marilynn. After graduating from the Juilliard Conservatory of Music, Dick had put aside his aspiration to be a concert pianist to fully commit himself as a missionary. After completing his work at Fuller Theological Seminary and getting his master's degree in theology from Princeton, he went to San Jose, Costa Rica, as a professor of New Testament at the Seminario Biblico. He and his wife, Irene, also a professor, taught for forty years at that seminary. During his long career, God graciously provided Dick with many opportunities to use his musical gifts by performing concerts in the National Theatre of Costa Rica as well as other Latin America capitals. But all that was in the future. Right now, Marilynn desperately wanted to meet Dick, hear him perform, and possibly play some two-piano numbers with him. She didn't hesitate as much as a quarter note when Jim invited her to come home with him after she learned that Dick would also be home from Fuller.

Marilynn was dazzled by Dick's amazing piano skills, and she was thrilled to be able to play several two-piano numbers as well as a solo number that she had polished for her own recital several years before. Jim began to wonder if he had made a mistake to expose his girlfriend to the charm and wit of his older, gifted brother. The more Dick's playing mesmerized Marilynn, the more deflated and sulky Jim became. He suffered even more mental anguish when Marilynn laughingly referred to her sulking suitor as Old Sobersides.

In the midst of Jim's self-pity, Mother Foulkes, who subscribed to Ben Franklin's proverb that honesty is the best policy, commented sweetly to Marilynn: "I don't know why Jim wants to go down and see his girlfriend in Mississippi when he knows such a nice girl like you right here."

A good son is not supposed to strangle his mother. Jim was a good son. He strangled his feelings instead. But he couldn't believe his mother would blurt out a statement like that.

Jim had no idea what impact his mother's remark would have on Marilynn, and he feared the worst. He was delighted, however, when he saw that it had broken Dick's spell over Marilynn and aroused that most human of all emotions, jealousy. She had to face the reality that she might lose out to the Southern belle.

Soon afterwards, Jim externed at a mission hospital in the mountains of Eastern Kentucky in Pikeville. While there, he received letters from both Mississippi and Columbus, Ohio.

The Southern belle kept assuring Jim of her undying love. Marilynn, on the other hand, wrote with great depth of feeling, often including a poem that she had written. To Marilynn, the word "love" was too precious to use before its time had arrived. But to Jim, the time had arrived. He had made the decision that Marilynn was the true love of his life.

Ever the gentleman, Jim felt that he at least owed it to the now-former girlfriend to tell her face-to-face why he was ending their relationship. Jim then informed Marilynn why he was going to make one more trip to Mississippi. But Marilynn did not seem reassured. She had no choice, however, but to wait and pray.

# Love and Marriage

Jim tried to make the breakup in Mississippi as easy as possible, but his mind was made up. It was over. He couldn't fake feelings he didn't feel. The long trip back to Columbus was made short by knowing who awaited him at the end of his journey.

As soon as he arrived home, Jim called Marilynn. He told her that he wanted to talk to her as soon as possible—*alone*—and Marilynn quickly consented. When they rendezvoused, Jim told her he had made a permanent break with his former Southern girlfriend.

There was no bolt of lightning this time, but Marilynn fell into Jim's waiting arms. Two hearts, bursting with love, were beating in rhythm. It was a story as old as creation itself: Eve once again had returned to the side of Adam.

Not so convinced, however, was Marilynn's mother. She didn't want this young adventurous doctor dragging her only child off to Africa. Why couldn't they marry and stay home, living comfortably on Jim's physician salary and moving up in society, as dictated by the prestige afforded a physician? But that was not what Jim and Marilynn wanted. They believed they had been called to serve in Africa. They did, at least, have the blessing of Marilynn's father in that decision.

Marilynn and Jim were married in a large church wedding in Toledo, in June of 1955, with Jim Diller serving as the best man. Surrounded by both sets of parents and a large group of IVCF friends, Jim and Marilynn said their vows. The only slip was Jim nervously saying, "with this *wing* I thee wed." Marilynn smiled as Jim slipped the ring on her finger. Then they were off in a rain of rice in their auto, bound for a honeymoon cottage in Ontario.

While on their honeymoon, they decided to visit Campus-in-the-Woods, where two of Jim's friends were on the IVCF training camp staff. It was one of those seemingly casual decisions that, in retrospect, made a huge impact on the direction of their lives.

# ChapterSeven
## "So Send I You"

**D**r. Robert L. Foster, a medical missionary in Northern Rhodesia (later Zambia) was on his first furlough. A man of prayer, he had asked God to give him a doctor and five nurses who would come to Africa to serve in the bush hospital he had built and opened three years earlier.

Serving as the doctor of the month at Campus-in-the-Woods, he knew full well that he would meet Christian students seriously considering the will of God for their lives. It seems he had hit pay dirt! Jim and Marilynn only had to spend a few hours talking with the dynamic Dr. Bob and his charming wife, Belva, before being convinced that Northern Rhodesia was the place they should serve. After talking it over between themselves that evening, they both felt a sense of peace and rightness about joining Dr. Foster at the Kaonde Hospital (later Mukinge).

"That was a great gift of God to us to have our place of service shown to us just as we were starting our life together," Jim said.

Following their honeymoon, Marilynn went back for her last year of nursing school and Jim started his general internship at Mt. Carmel Hospital in Columbus. Although they lived in a tiny apartment on the edge of campus, they saw very little of one another during that first year. They both left the apartment at 6:30 A.M., and Jim had to work every other night. Marilynn contracted infectious mononucleosis, causing her to miss so many of her classes that she didn't have enough credits to graduate in June. Nevertheless, in August 1956, she graduated with honors, summa cum laude. Her bulky graduation gown covered the baby bulge nicely; she was five months' pregnant.

Jim had already begun his surgical residency at Akron General Hospital in June. He and Marilynn now worshipped at the Goss Memorial Church, which provided them with a temporary home.

The church emphasized missions, and Akron General had seven other house doctors besides Jim who were missionary candidates. Several of the staff doctors were very sympathetic to the residents who would use their skills to help the poor in the Third World. The chief of surgery encouraged the staff surgeons to give the young men heading overseas as much experience as possible during their stay (which might only be for eighteen months or two years).

While at Akron General, Jim met a fellow resident, Lowell Gess, who had already spent one term in West Africa. Gess freely shared with the other residents the lessons that he had learned while in Africa. One had nothing to do with medicine, but it was an area that Jim always enjoyed—hunting.

Gess insisted that Jim take with him a .300 Weatherby Magnum rifle to keep meat on the table. Sleeping sickness spread by tsetse flies surrounding Mukinge made it impossible for domestic animals to survive. That meant that Jim would have to hunt elephants and hippos in order to supply meat for the hospital; they would rely on the abundant antelope for their own needs. Gess, who would complete a residency in ophthalmology, would later teach Jim the basics of eye surgery when they met again in Sierra Leon.

Before leaving Akron for Africa, the name Jim Elliot would once again be emblazoned on Jim's mind. One day the banner headline in the Akron *Beacon Journal* screamed out the news of five martyrs killed by the Auca Indians in Ecuador. A surgeon that Jim was assisting that morning commented what a great loss it was for five gifted young men with their lives ahead of them to be killed. Jim emphatically informed the surgeon that the five missionaries had not died in vain, adding that the blood of the martyrs was the seed of the church. The only response the surgeon could make was, "Uh, OK, Foulkes. I didn't mean to upset you."

Jim saw the first inkling of how Jim Elliot's death would multiply the number of missionaries abroad. Four of his fellow residents were Wheaton College graduates who were friends of Elliot. The news of his death affected them profoundly.

One of the four had turned his back on God and had dropped out of church. His godly wife had asked the other residents to pray for her backslidden husband. The young doctor was so moved by Elliot's death as well as that of his classmate, Ed McCully, that he recommitted his life and went out as a medical missionary to South America with the Missionary Aviation Fellowship (MAF). "He beat all the rest of us to the mission field," Jim said.

Before Jim and his bride could leave for the remote regions of Northern Rhodesia, they would have to face the same difficult problem that all missionaries going out with faith missions face: collecting a support team to undergird their ministry with prayer and finances.

For Jim, it was somewhat humiliating. He was cast from the same mold as his father, conservative and self reliant. (Billy Foulkes was also generous. In his later years he gave away 50 percent of his salary to the Lord's work.)

"It was a salutary test of humility for a professional person to start begging for his bread and butter," Jim recalled. The South Africa General Mission (SAGM) was a faith mission. A missionary could not leave for the field until full support was raised, regarded as a seal of the Lord's calling.

Jim soon stopped viewing the seeking of support as begging. After all, the first missionary to the Gentiles (Paul) made it clear that the gifts given him were really a fragrant offering, an acceptable sacrifice, pleasing to God (Phil. 4:18 NIV). And did not Jesus say, "It is more blessed to give than to receive" (Acts 20:35)? Instead of begging for money, Jim was giving his team (as he called his supporters) an opportunity to offer up a fragrant offering to God.

"The first gift that I got from a young lady was a small amount, but it was a holy offering," Jim recalled. A total of five churches and many friends would follow the young lady, pledging their support for the Foulkeses. Jim followed the faith principle of legendary missionary Hudson Taylor of not mentioning a specific need unless asked personally, "What are your needs?"

In the final analysis, it was prayer that enabled Jim and his family to go to the mission field and stay there for thirty-eight years. But he never was truly at ease accepting gifts. "Being a faithful steward of sanctified money is a heavy responsibility," he explained. "It weighs on your conscious enough that I felt more comfortable when we were broke because of fuel costs needed to teach two distant Bible classes in the bush each week rather than when we had some money left over at the end of the year." But Jim found a rich blessing in learning to depend on God to supply all of his needs. That simple act of trust caused him to become much better acquainted with Jehovah-Jireh, the God who provides. And Jehovah-Jireh provided the needed full support for Jim and Marilynn in just six months!

When the apostle Paul left for his first missionary journey with Barnabas, the church at Antioch commended them to the work by prayer and the laying on of hands (Acts 13:3). Jim and Marilynn followed the New Testament pattern before leaving for Africa. A solemn but moving commissioning service was held in the Goss Memorial Church where the couple had worshipped during their eighteen months in Akron.

Dr. and Mrs. Don Duckles, special friends of the Foulkes, sang "So Send I You." Pastor Troup placed his hands on the kneeling couple and commended them to the Lord as the missionary-minded congregation joined in silent prayer. (Sadly, Pastor Troup's daughter, Janette, who was a fellow resident with Jim at Akron General, would die of Lassa Fever at her mission hospital in Nigeria. Her touching story is told in the book *Fever*.)

Jim would long meditate on the text from which the song title was taken: "As the Father has sent me, so send I you." The Father sent the Son knowing that He would be tortured and put to death. Jim pondered seriously what was involved in his Master's commission. He concluded that they were being sent out in the same way. Whatever the cost, they were wiling to pay it. They were in God's good hands—under His wing, the safest of all places.

Now they were ready to leave home and family for the place of their calling. But something life-changing had happened to them in Akron. A daughter, Terrie Lynn, had been born on December 22, 1956.

"Our daughter Terrie made life so much more complete and increased our love for each other greatly," Jim recalled.

Soon a second blessing followed. Marilynn gave birth to a son, David Evan, in April of 1958. It was a day of rejoicing for both, but especially for Jim, who felt both thrilled and fulfilled as he cuddled his baby boy in his arms.

The two who had become one were now leaving for Africa as four—with love for one another and for God.

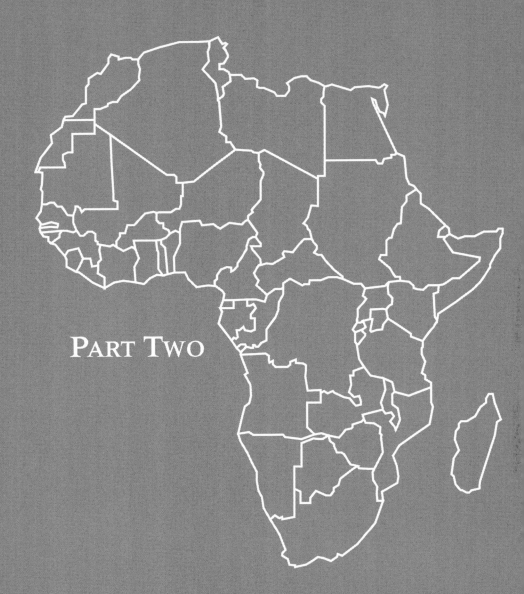

PART TWO

# ChapterEight
## Mukinge Welcome

**D**r. Bob Foster drove over the bumpy dirt roads of Northern Rhodesia the same way he practiced medicine—with gusto and intensity. Jim and Marilynn, with two babies in arms, clung to their car seats as best they could as the gung ho missionary doctor fishtailed around towering anthills while trying to dodge the deep bone-jolting holes that pockmarked the narrow dirt road.

Jim and Marilynn, mouths dry and filled with the taste of the gritty dust that had also colored red every inch of their clothing and exposed skin, still listened intently over the roar of the motor as Dr. Foster regaled them with the history of Mukinge.

Dr. Bob—as he was usually called—was the son of Rev. Charles and June Foster, the pioneer missionaries who founded Mukinge Hill Station. In 1917, Charles and his new wife had to walk for three weeks from the railhead in Northern Rhodesia, along with more than one hundred carriers, to arrive in the northwestern part of the country. They started a primitive mission station called Musonweji. Their son, Robert, was born in 1924.

Two years later, the Foster family moved to Mukinge Hill close to the government center at Kasempa. They had come to take the good news of the gospel of Jesus Christ to the Kaonde tribe. It was a fertile field for missionaries. At that point in time, the entire district could boast not one confessing Christian!

A brilliant linguist, Charles Foster translated the New Testament and, along with others, the Old Testament into the Kikaonde language that had never before been put into writing. But the beloved *Bwana* (white man) was determined that the Kaonde would hear the Word of God in their own language. He was convinced that only the Word of God could free the Kaonde people from the dark powers of witchcraft that had them enslaved.

*David Mukimwa and Rev. Charles Foster receiving the first copies of the complete Kaonde Bible. This was a lifelong labor of love for our pioneer missionary. In a later ceremony, Rev. Foster delivered a copy of the Bible to President Kaunda.*

The lack of medical care and the high death rate of infants—including that of their own two-year-old daughter—created a burden in the hearts of the Fosters to have a medical doctor at the Mukinge station. They prayed fervently to God to send them one. Little did they realize that God had already answered their prayers with the birth of their fourth child, Robert Livingstone Foster. (Named, rather significantly, after the beloved pioneer, David Livingstone.)

Bob actually grew up in faraway Canada, separated from his parents by distance and by World War II. He graduated from the University of Toronto Medical College in 1947. A year later, he married Belva Mark, an English major at the University of Toronto who also felt that God was calling her to missionary service in Africa. Both were officially accepted by the South African General Mission shortly after their wedding.

Bob arrived with Belva and their one-year-old son, Stephen, at Mukinge as a full-fledged medical doctor in 1950. Dr. Bob was a magnetic speaker. In a short eight-month blitz, the Lord used his persuasive speaking to raise enough funds for the family's personal support and for ten tons of medical supplies—beds, tables, drugs, surgical instruments—indeed everything needed to equip a forty-bed hospital. Alas, however, not a dime was raised for the building! That minor omission did not diminish the dynamic faith of the young doctor. He simply set up shop in a mud-and-grass clinic until his dream hospital materialized.

"Well, we're here!" Dr. Bob announced in his booming voice to the weary passengers as he pulled off the dirt road onto the Mukinge Hospital grounds. To the exhausted but excited young couple, Mukinge looked like a gem in its picturesque setting between two towering hills, an emerald green oasis in the dusty brown of the surrounding bush country.

Mukinge Hospital consists of a series of single story buildings linked to each other by outdoor concrete walkways covered with tin roofing and leading to various wards. The mission station now sits on a one-thousand-acre site and includes a secondary boarding school for five hundred students and a nurses' training school.

According to Dr. Bob Foster's biography, *Sword and Scalpel*, his father had chosen Mukinge Hill as the site for the new mission station for a variety of practical reasons: "Located more than four thousand feet above sea level, it would provide a more temperate climate than the lowlands; springs in the valley provided an abundant water supply; the nearby *boma* (local seat of government) would expedite business." (Information on the history of Mukinge Hill Station is based on Dr. Bob Foster's biography, *Sword and Scalpel*, written by Lorry Lutz.

Much to the delight of the missionaries, Chief Kasempa said he would be delighted to have the mission station located near his capital. And the British colonial authorities made an offer the missionaries couldn't refuse: They would lease them the one thousand acres for just a pound a year!

Bob and Belva warmly welcomed Jim and Marilynn and their two small children into their home, thereby easing the culture shock involved in leaving behind the soft American way of life to embrace a rugged Rhodesian lifestyle.

The indefatigable Dr. Bob lost no time in orienting his raw recruits to the medical realities of a bush hospital. Most of the patients had placed their faith in the magical cure of a ñanga (witch doctor). To the local populace, the spirit (i.e., demonic) world was as real—maybe even more so—than the natural world. They believed that physical sickness always has a supernatural origin. Thus it logically followed that a cure would have to come from the same source.

These traditional beliefs have extended long past the arrival of medical technology, with some humorous results, as when patients lying on the X-ray table for a chest film would jump off of the table when they heard the whir of the machine taking the picture. They were convinced that the mysterious equipment, combined with the strange noise, had driven out the bad spirits that had invaded their chests. The whirring machine employed by the white doctor soon became a preferred method of chasing away evil spirits because it was a lot faster and less painful than the traditional techniques used by the local ñanga.

In those techniques, the tribal doctor, after seeking a second opinion from his spirit guide, would make deep cuts on the painful part of the chest. Next, he would heat up an animal horn on a fire and put the open end over the cuts. The blood and serum drawn out of the cuts by the vacuum in the horn supposedly sucked out the evil spirit by the time the horn cooled and fell off. The telltale round tattoo left behind by the hot horn was a permanent marker of the procedure.

Dr. Foster's practice of modern medicine was reinforced by his vigorous bedside manner. When he picked up his syringe, looked the patient straight in the eye, and in his loud voice told the patient that this injection was going to cure him, the patient had no alternative but to get well. The white doctor's "magic" was hard to match, going a long way past the placebo effect of his persuasive personality. Countless times, just a couple of shots of penicillin were seen to cure serious pneumonia in a child. The villagers soon learned that Western medicine healed the ill better than the witch doctor's ritual involving bones, herbs, and roots.

Surgery was considered an even more unbelievable feat. In his first years at the hospital, Dr. Foster removed countless ovarian cysts, some weighing as much as thirty or forty pounds. There was no Zambian Academy of Medicine prohibiting physicians to advertise, so Dr. Foster publicly displayed the oversized cysts in the hospital during visiting hours like a gardener entering prize heads of cabbage at a county fair.

Soon his fame became so widespread in the area that his grateful patients dubbed him "Ba Kahaya"—the name of a famous witch doctor. That fame came after the successful procedure to reverse the infertility of the paramount chief's number one wife. Years later, speaking to an audience at a medical conference, Jim caused great amusement by innocently stating that Dr. Foster had won the confidence of the villagers by "quickly getting the paramount chief's wife pregnant"!

Nevertheless, "to be esteemed of God" was always Dr. Bob's primary motivation. He emphasized healing of the soul as well as the body. He insisted that the local church and community be involved in the hospital, and that the hospital be a center of evangelism. The aggressive missionary's daring faith continually amazed Jim.

"Once I observed Bob ordering an expensive generator for the hospital without the slightest idea as to how it would be paid for," he recalled. "But his response always was, 'God will provide.' He was akin in spirit to Hudson Taylor who declared: 'Depend on it, God's work done in God's way will never lack God's supply.'"

Jim soon learned that his medical mentor would sometimes rush in where angels fear to tread, and Jim found himself on the side of the angels one day when it came time to flush out a wounded leopard from the high grass around a nearby local village.

*Dr. Bob and Belva Foster. He returned to Zambia to found Mukinge Hospital fifty miles from where he was born. He is currently founding his fourth hospital with his son, Dr. Stephen Foster.*

At 6:00 A.M. one day, just weeks after the Foulkes family had arrived at Mukinge, a runner from the nearby leprosy village came charging into the hospital compound. After catching his breath, the excited runner said that his village was being terrorized by a leopard that had been shot and wounded, but not killed.

In the middle of the night, the leopard had jumped onto the grass roof of one of the huts. The man inside the hut blasted off his muzzle loader rifle, up through the thatch where the big cat was rapidly clawing through. To the great relief of the frantic hut occupants, the wounded animal leapt down and ran away. The ten or twelve inches of grass thatch supported by thin poles was all that had separated them from the hungry leopard. It would have only taken the beast a few more seconds to have broken through the roof.

Frozen with fear, clutching his ancient muzzle loader, the man finally got up enough nerve to unlatch his door and look out. He could see several other men in the village who also had ventured out. They all agreed that the shot apparently had scared off the deadly intruder—until, that is, they heard a low moan that seemed to emanate from a nearby clump of high grass. They immediately knew that the injured cat, nursing its wounds only twenty-five yards away, was putting them all in jeopardy. So they dispatched the frightened messenger, who literally ran for his life to the mission hospital for help.

Within an hour, a small but heavily armed posse left the station for the village. Dr. Bob had his .303, another missionary, Dave Fields, carried his .30-06. A Kaonde employee, known to be a crack shot, brought his muzzle loader. Totally confused as to what was the best weapon for such an occasion, Jim brought his own arsenal—a .300 Weatherby Magnum rifle, a shotgun, and his .38 pistol.

When the men arrived, the terrified villagers were huddled around a big fire. Two of the men had muzzle loaders, the rest had long spears. They quickly pointed to an area of high elephant grass, about twenty-by-twenty square yards and six feet high. Visibility was only two feet. That would not even give a hunter enough time to get his weapon up to his shoulder and pull the trigger if the cat charged. The hapless victim would only have time to see a flash of yellow fur before he felt the fangs close on his throat.

Jim remembered reading stories about professional hunters in similar circumstances who would crawl into a thicket to kill a

*The hero who ended the threat of this wounded leopard.*

leopard that their client had wounded. The hunter would tie his thick woolen sweater around his neck so that if the cat attacked by going for the jugular, the animal would be rewarded only with a mouth full of wool. That was the theory anyway—not one that Jim was interested in testing. In fact, his mouth was so dry that he didn't have enough saliva to lick a postage stamp. He was, as he put it, "literally scared spitless."

The armed men had surrounded the thicket, standing about ten feet away from the high grass, so that when the leopard came out they would be able to see his last leap and get a quick shot off. They yelled at the top of their voices, trying to scare the leopard out of the high grass. When that didn't work, they fired a few shots into the center of the thicket—still no response. Then it dawned on them that firing squads always stand in a line, not a circle.

It was now time for Plan B. Dr. Bob quickly took command. "Men," he shouted, "when I count five we're all going in!"

Jim made a split-second decision. "Count me out!" he called out loud and clear. (Dave Fields later told Jim he really appreciated his "chickening out" so quickly. He said that he, too, had already made up his mind. He was not about to wade into a thicket of six-foot-high elephant grass to try kicking up a wounded leopard as if it were a jack rabbit.)

Plan C was now proposed by their Zambian colleague, a seasoned hunter. Having noticed a slight breeze blowing, he said he believed he could get a fire going even if the grass was pretty green that early in the dry season. After several attempts, the grass finally caught fire with a loud crackle. The billowing smoke coming from the slow-burning brush obviously posed a threat to the lurking leopard.

Suddenly, the men heard a loud roar, which surprised them because lions are supposed to roar just before a charge, but not leopards. This leopard was playing by its own rules. The big cat lunged out of the thicket directly in front of the Zambian, who had wisely already put his muzzle loader up to his shoulder in the firing position.

He instinctively aimed and fired at the chest of the cat flying in his direction. The leopard's last leap didn't quite carry it to his quarry. It crumpled to the ground in a dead heap, only a step away from the cool hunter.

The three missionaries rejoiced to see the seasoned pro demonstrate his marksmanship, rather than putting their own shooting skills to the test.

The intense fear of the village was now transformed into exuberant joy that immediately erupted into loud shouting and dancing. The men from the mission were instant heroes, but they transferred the glory all to God.

Jim concluded, "I have always considered that my cowardice might well have saved Bob Foster's life."

# ChapterNine
## Initiation to Sleeping Sickness

The Kafue National Park is located nearby in the rugged bush country and it is a veritable ark, teeming with herds of puku, impala, roan, sable, eland, kudu, elephant, and virtually the whole range of African big game.

A friendly game ranger, Johnny Uys, offered to give Jim and Marilynn a tour of the Busanga flood plains. This massive grassland area of the park would give them a closer look at the huge herds of animals that grazed there. That invitation was quickly accepted by the newly arrived missionaries. The game ranger drove them around in an old, battered Land Rover.

They eventually came upon a mass of grazing Cape buffalo. The ranger suddenly revved up his engine, careening like a kamikaze driver straight toward the herd of nine hundred monster buffalo. Jim and Marilynn held their breath as the Land Rover drew closer and closer to the big animals who did not seem inclined to share their space with a puny four-wheeler.

At the last instant, the herd cracked open just enough to allow the Land Rover to get through. But the terrified passengers found themselves amidst a swirl of horns that could as easily bring death to a man as to a lion, horns so close they could have reached out and touched them.

"We didn't know whether to thank Johnny for this wild experience or throttle him," Jim said, sounding as if he favored the second option. Johnny became a good friend, and later, as the director of Game and Tsetse, offered to buy the fencing for Jim's proposed game farm. He was grieved by his many friends when, years later, he was killed by a bull elephant while leading a walking safari in Zimbabwe.

*The Busanga flood plains located forty-five miles from Mukinge. The nine hundred Cape buffalo that those pictured are watching aren't visible in this picture. A few minutes later they would have been, since Johnny Uys, the game ranger on the right, drove them in his Land Rover right through the middle of the huge herd. This is also where Marilynn was bitten by tsetse flies and contracted sleeping sickness.*

But a bigger scare was yet to come. For the people of Kasempa, there were microscopic enemies that could be just as deadly as man-eating animals.

Ten days after returning from their little jaunt through the game park, Marilynn spiked a fever and developed a red, raised patch on her forehead. After two days of unremitting fevers, Marilynn's temperature climbed to 106 degrees, with no response at all to anti-malarial drugs.

Jim grew worried that he might lose his life partner. He prayed, and the answer came in the person of Dr. Bob, who returned from a trip in the nick of time. Within minutes, he examined the red lesion, recognized it as a trypanosomal chancre (the result of a bite by an infected tsetse fly), and immediately began the life-saving treatment.

At that point in time, Jim knew almost nothing about Rhodesian sleeping sickness. Through the years, however, he would garner experience in treating more than one thousand cases. With the tsetse fly on the wing, Jim found himself practicing medicine at the epicenter of a huge sleeping-sickness belt.

The tsetse fly looks innocent enough, but it requires a blood meal to survive and, when hungry, it will attack any exposed skin with a vengeance and even has no trouble in biting through a thin shirt. If the fly's probe (proboscis) hits a nerve on the way in, it feels much like a hot needle. At the least, the victim ends up with an itchy bite. The worst outcome occurs if the fly injects a parasite into its victim before withdrawing its blood meal. This microscopic invader, called a trypanosome, moves from the blood to eventually invade the brain. This stage progresses to drowsiness, then coma, and finally death if untreated. Hence the common name, African sleeping sickness.

It is Mukinge that is at the center of a twenty-mile diameter tsetse-free area, which allows it to support a human population. Mukinge would have more sleeping sickness patients in its wards than any other hospital in the country. This gave Jim the opportunity to share his experience in the clinical aspects of the disease by publishing articles in tropical medicine journals. The most effective treatment for the second stage of the disease (invariably fatal if untreated, given its very lethal strains) was plain old rat poison.

"We treated hundreds of those suffering from this dread disease by pumping rat poison (arsenic) into their veins," Jim recalled. "The prognostic rule was all too accurate: If you walked into the hospital for treatment, you walked out. If you were carried into the hospital, you would be carried out—in a coffin!"

After recovering from her sleeping sickness (first stage), Marilynn immediately enrolled in Belva Foster's school on how to cook for a family in the tropical bush.

She and Jim began their Kikaonde language training taught by Bob's father, the Reverend C. S. Foster. The pioneer missionary, a brilliant linguist, was always addressed by the respectful title of Bwana by everyone who knew him. Marilynn proved to be the prize pupil for the old Bwana. He was still trying to codify the difficult tonal system of the language, and Marilynn was the ideal person to help him since she had almost perfect pitch.

Marilynn could easily detect the crucial spot when the second syllable of a word would slide up a quarter of a step, making the word mean something entirely different. The language class turned into a lab where the informant would pronounce a word and the Bwana would ask, "up or down or the same?"

They all sounded the same to Jim's tin ear, and he quickly became bored. "I wanted to be focusing on the basics of the language rather than the fine points," Jim said.

He had been attending the language classes for only a few weeks when relief came. Dr. Bob had to leave the hospital to conduct weekend preaching missions in all of the medical schools in South Africa. That meant that Jim had to discontinue his intensive language study in order to spend most of his day in the hospital. But he had a private tutor in Marilynn, who both encouraged and corrected him.

"Just as important as the medical therapies, all of our patients were covered in prayer. Most staff, including the surgeons, nurses, and chaplains, prayed with the patients. Communicating with the hurting ones, be it patients or families, required fluency in their 'heart language,'" Jim said.

The final language exam told the tale: Marilynn received the highest grade anyone had ever gotten in the Bwana's exam, while

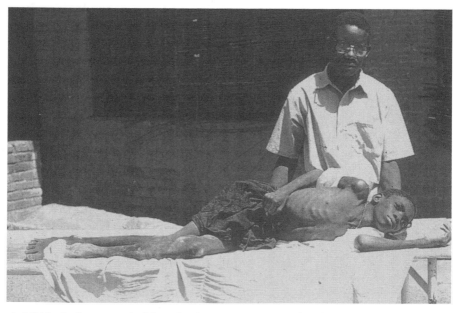

*A child in the late stage of African sleeping sickness is pictured with Yoba Joseph, the hospital secretary. Joseph is the first living child of Kyabasonga.*

Jim distinguished himself by getting the lowest grade ever to still count as a pass.

But pass he did. Fortunately, the best way to learn a language is to live among the people who speak it. Jim, too, would eventually be conversing with his patients, and even teaching and preaching in Kikaonde.

# ChapterTen
## Bush Medicine

T he young American doctor soon learned that practicing medicine in a tropical jungle was a world away and a century behind the way it was done in the United States. He had to cope with a host of tropical diseases that doctors in the U.S. never see—malaria, African sleeping sickness, small pox, and rabies, to mention a few.

Africans living in the bush share their habitat with wild animals. This exposes them to continual danger from venomous snakes, hippos (who kill more people than any other animal on the continent), lions, leopards, elephants, crocodiles, and Cape buffalo.

But one of the biggest threats to life and limb is man-made fire. With thatched roofs and open campfires in every village, serious burns are a common problem. Epileptic children who didn't take their anti-convulsive medicine regularly were at high risk. Tragically, they often fell face down into the fire.

"Those kids would barely have healed up their skin grafts from a previous fit before arriving at the hospital with a fresh set of new burns," Jim recalled. He marveled how the Creator put such a fantastic protective reflex into the eyelids. "The lids always closed to protect the eye before the child's face actually hit the fire. The eye itself is saved but the eyelids are deeply burned and will slough."

The race to graft skin from behind the ear and replace the burned-off lids before eyes were damaged from exposure was intense. Failure meant permanent blindness.

Second-degree burns over the body from scalding were also commonplace and difficult to treat. The hospital didn't have a bank of artificial skin to cover fresh burns. God, however, had provided for their needs in the placenta of women. Washed placental amniotic tissue proved effective as a skin covering since the thin membrane stuck well to the burn, preventing infection and fluid

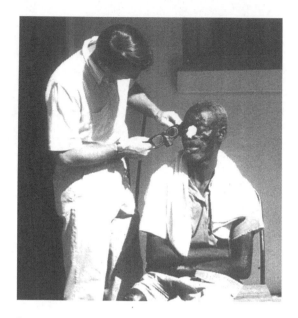

*Dr. Dick Furman is ready to do the final fitting for a prosthesis that he made from fiberglass to replace this man's nose. It had been completely destroyed by yaws twenty years earlier. Resident artist, Juliet Baker (who painted the cover for this book), painted the prosthesis to exactly match the skin color.*

loss. Even full thickness burns (burns that involve damage to both skin layers, plus underlying tissue, muscle, bone, or organs) benefitted from this early skin covering prior to skin grafting.

After the arrival of AIDS in Zambia, however, that treatment had to be discontinued. The virus invaded the amniotic layer, exposing the patient to the possibility of infection with HIV. Thus, an inexpensive and effective skin covering that had prevented infection in many burn patients was no longer available.

The general rule was that if a patient had more than 30 percent of his skin surface burned, it was unlikely that he would survive. That rule was put to the test when three teenagers arrived at the hospital with at least 40 percent of their bodies seared with fire.

The Christian boys had been making bricks for a church project when a grass fire got out of control. Surrounded by ten-foot-tall flames, the boys had to make a difficult decision—stand where they were and be cooked alive or run for it and be burned. They ran screaming through the flames.

The lower half of their bodies suffered full thickness burns. "They really needed to be in an intensive care burn center in Capetown. But their care fell to us. We tried our best," Jim said, in recalling the incident.

The young patients were given heavy doses of narcotics each morning to diminish the pain. Then they were put in a huge metal whirlpool and scrubbed by a physical therapist to remove the debris that had collected on their burns during the previous day. Their wounds were then dried and lathered with silvadene ointment and treated without dressings under bed cradles. They were given around-the-clock antibiotics and fluids.

Jim and the staff knew they were in a race with time. Unless a significant percentage of the boys' open wounds were grafted within thirty days, the boys would die of infection. The teenagers had to be taken numerous times to the operating room where the hospital staff tried to get as many as possible of the partial thickness skin grafts to "take."

"We lost the race with two of the boys." Jim said years later, still able to recall the timing of their death. "One lad died on day twenty-seven and the other on day twenty-nine. The third boy was almost surely going to make it, but he got depressed. He was sure that he would soon join his two friends."

A young British physical therapist working with him knew that just a touch from Jesus, the Great Physician, would bring about both spiritual and physical healing. She spent hours with him massaging and moving his joints and praying for his recovery.

"Her prayers were answered and he turned the corner," Jim said, obviously relishing the memory.

A year later, the young man walked into the hospital outpatient department to announce that he felt a call from God to follow in his father's footsteps and be a preacher. The whole staff rejoiced that at least one of the three who had literally gone through the fire had survived to spread the gospel. He would indeed some day see his two friends again—in glory.

There was never a shortage of patients at Mukinge. Statistics tell why. The hospital served 50,000 people in a two-hundred-mile radius. The outpatient clinic alone would see 200 to 250 patients daily. Charge nurse Marge Harstine (also an Ohio State grad) ran the outpatient clinic like a marine top sergeant: filling out medical forms, shuttling patients into the proper examining rooms, and writing for treatments. She also scolded mothers for not bringing their children in sooner for medicine—but her soft side came out as frequently when she would gently cuddle a crying baby in her arms. In the same persona, she was "Auntie Marge" to all the children at the station, and especially to Jim and Marilynn's girls.

In the early days, the entire hospital staff knew that no matter how much they extended themselves, one grim statistic remained: a rural family living more than twenty miles from the hospital could expect to lose 50 percent of their children from lack of proper medical care. Unlike in the developed world there were no emergency ambulances that could travel twenty miles in twenty minutes on paved roads.

Accompanied by a visitor on one of his morning rounds in the wards, Jim stopped to check on a twelve-year-old boy lying on a cot, with his mother sitting beside him. The lad was in the last stages of a futile struggle with cancer of the kidney.

"This kid has had two courses of chemotherapy, but the cure rate for this kind of cancer is poor. If he had gotten diagnosed earlier, we might have saved him, but he came in too late," Jim said sadly. That was a statement one heard over and over again at Mukinge Hospital—"We got them too late."

The major diseases that kill millions of African children each year are malaria, pneumonia, dysentery, measles, and malnutrition, with

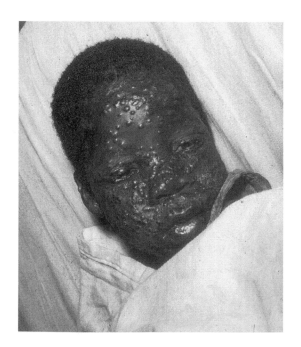

*Small pox epidemic, 1959, which had a 50 percent mortality rate.*

*An entire ward was required for malnourished children with Kwashiorkor. One special student was Irene Kasambira, who now has a master's degree in nursing. She lives in Peoria, Illinois, with her husband, Paul, who is a university professor.*

AIDS numbers climbing up alarmingly. Because of ineffective public health programs, poorly equipped and staffed hospitals, and late arrivals at the hospital, the health of Africa's children has improved only marginally in the past twenty years. In Africa's many war-torn countries, the health services virtually collapse and the health of children has no priority at all.

The inevitable result of treatment overuse combined with the wiles of a very adaptable parasite came in the rapid development of chloroquine-resistant malaria. The first sign that chloroquine was losing the battle with the mosquito-borne disease was a dramatic rise in the hospital's monthly death rate, up from an average of four or five to more than double that.

The number of children with malaria exploded at Mukinge, partly because the eleven government-operated clinics in the district had been sending their worst cases to the mission hospital. The clinics were still treating the youngsters with chloroquine, the only drug supplied to them. The resistant parasites moved into the brains in some of the young victims, causing cerebral malaria, the most deadly form of the disease. The under-treated children would lapse into unconsciousness.

# To Africa with Love

The clinics had no vehicles to transport their patients, and it often took a day or two for them to even find a vehicle that could be used as an ambulance. By the time the children arrived at Mukinge, they often had been unconscious for two or three days. It was the same old story—they had arrived too late.

Anemia is another feared feature of the deadly disease. The new strains of the malaria parasite destroyed the red-blood cells much more savagely than before, increasing the need for life-saving blood transfusions. Several of the alkaloid derivatives from a Chinese plant became the drugs of choice for oral treatment. But a course of these refined derivatives (such as ACT) could cost in the range of twenty times the cost of a course of chloroquine. So medical workers found themselves facing a dilemma: do you use cheap drugs that you know don't work well, or do you use a drug that does work well, but is only affordable for a relatively small number of your patients? It's a question with no easy answer, and one which they continue to face with other deadly diseases.

During his routine rounds on the inpatient wards, Jim often found patients with difficult diagnostic problems. But none as bizarre as the case of the lion-eating man.

Jim had just settled into his favorite chair and closed his eyes to relax, when there came a desperate knock on the door. A good friend and church worker, Elizabeth Kibanza, entered the room, obviously in deep distress. She blurted out that she had just brought her brother to the hospital, and she was afraid that he was going to die. Jim bolted out of the chair and ran down the red trail leading to the hospital.

He found a man writhing in agony, the skin across his abdomen stretched as tightly as a drum. His vital signs were so poor that Jim feared that he was another person who had waited too long before coming to the hospital.

Profoundly dehydrated, the patient's vomiting and high tinkling bowel sounds pointed to a total bowel obstruction. Jim alerted the surgical crew to prepare for an emergency operation, knowing that Doraine Ross, Mukinge matron and head of surgery, would have her team and all the needed instruments ready to go in record time.

# Bush Medicine

*The bush ambulance. Even today, some distant patients arrive on litters strapped between two bicycles.*

The looks on the faces of the medical staff as they rehydrated him showed that they had little hope for the patient. Elizabeth, a deaconess at the Mutanda Central Church who had been praying for twenty years for her brother's salvation, now prayed more fervently than ever.

After administering anesthesia, Jim made the needed incision. Further exploration revealed the site of the obstruction in the small bowel. The involved area was stretched as taut as a balloon. After opening the site of the obstruction, Jim couldn't believe what he was seeing. It looked as if the man's bowel had been obstructed by a piece of rug. A closer look, however, along with a bit of cleansing, revealed that the rug was actually a hunk of animal skin!

Jim removed the furry object and then did a bowel resection and anastomosis. The patient hovered between life and death for several days. But the seventh day he was well on his way to recovery.

Then he told the rest of the story.

He had been having stomachaches for some time, so he went to see the local witch doctor. The ñanga consulted his spirit guides and divined that his client would be cured if he would swallow a piece of lion skin, washed down with a potion that he had concocted.

The man made two valiant attempts to swallow the furry skin, but the reflexes in the back of his throat kicked in, making it impossible for him to swallow his lion's share. Finally, the man got dead drunk and, with his wife pushing it down his throat, the skin passed the first barrier.

"Rather miraculously, the fur got through his esophagus and even through his stomach," Jim said. The furry medicine negotiated the first two feet of the small bowel and then it came to a sudden and permanent stop. It would not budge another inch.

"The obstruction would have consigned him to an early death if it were not for the emergency surgery." With a straight face, Jim noted, "This lion-eating man almost earned the dubious distinction of being the first recorded death in which a lion had killed from the inside out."

The man's near-death experience caused him to come to his senses as he realized that his confidence in the dark powers of witchcraft had almost killed him. He confessed his sins to God and accepted His Son as his Savior. All of the surgical staff rejoiced with Elizabeth that her brother had come home from the far country like the biblical prodigal son. She had interceded for him in prayer for two decades, and now, like the father in the story, she could say to her family: "Celebrate and be glad, for this brother of yours was dead and is alive again, he was lost and is found" (Luke 15:32 NIV).

At times *in*gestion rather than *di*gestion caused some of the more difficult problems at Mukinge.

One young lady arrived at the hospital with terminal kidney failure. The medical staff concluded that she had ingested a lethal poison. (Many of the local plant poisons are toxic to the kidneys.)

The woman admitted that she had recently gone to her favorite witch doctor with a minor complaint and had dutifully swallowed the concoction that he gave her. Her angry family stormed back to the ñanga, demanding he show them what potion he had given her. Then they forced the witch doctor to drink his own medicine. He, too, went into severe renal failure, his kidneys shut down, and he died a week later.

One of the most feared diseases that Mukinge had to deal with almost annually was rabies. It was felt that the large wild jackal population kept the infection alive in the dogs of the district. The general rule is that once a human who has been bitten by a rabid dog starts to show the symptoms of rabies encephalitis, there is no hope for a cure.

It was very sad when the price of a vial of anti-rabies vaccine climbed to seventy dollars, since that priced it out of the affordable range for the under-developed world where rabies is a common problem.

Jim has a picture of a twelve-year-old boy who was in the last stages of the disease. As he went into the lad's room he found the boy's father sobbing. He was just in time to hear the dying boy comfort his father with the words, "Don't cry, Daddy. I'm just going to be with Jesus and I will see you later over there." That brought tears to Jim's eyes. What a difference it makes in death to know that you have eternal life.

The worst epidemic occurred in the late 1970s. After three people had died of rabies, even the general public realized that they had to do away with dogs that had not been vaccinated by the local

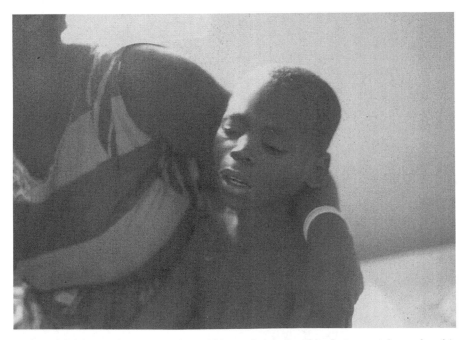

*A dear child dying of rabies. Jim visited him an hour after this photo was taken, when his father was holding him, and heard him try to comfort his father with the words, "Don't cry, Daddy. I'm just going to be with Jesus."*

vet officer. Jim remembered, "Anytime a dog entered the one thousand acres of the mission property, it was shot. We killed seventy-two dogs on the mission station alone."

After killing those seventy-two dogs, almost all of the men were out of shells. However, the rabid dogs still kept coming. Jim dug out his old hunting bow and started shooting them in the chest with his fiberglass arrows.

One afternoon while Jim was at work, a rabid dog charged into their yard and started attacking their dog. Marilynn immediately located the bow and ran out to defend her turf. She got a close shot and hit the stray dog in the chest, but not very deeply. With the arrow hanging limply at his side, he turned and came straight for Marilynn. She sprinted back to the house and just managed to slam the door in the face of the furious dog. A too-close encounter!

In another instance, Jim was with Milt Arnold when they were charged by a rabid dog near the hospital. Since they were both at work, they had no firearms. Milt had a club, so he bravely stood in front of Jim to stop the charge. In that situation they only had one chance, and if Milt missed the dog's head, they would be bitten for sure. With his adrenaline pumping full force, Milt brought his club down on his fast moving target and crushed his skull. No home-run hit could have been as satisfying as that.

The staff at Mukinge cared for all who came. Some were near death with life-threatening dysentery; some required emergency care for lethal snake bites. Some needed care for lion or leopard attacks, others needed amputation of limbs after suffering hippo or crocodile bites. Death was a common occurrence.

Before the advent of AIDS, it was always the little children that led the hit list. It was the high mortality rate of infants and children that reduced the average life span of the African people.

And the children of the missionaries were no exception, as the Foulkes family was to find out later.

# ChapterEleven
## David

Jim suspected malaria when his eighteen-month-old son, David, spiked a temperature of 105 degrees on a sunny Saturday morning at Mukinge. He took David over to the hospital and had lab technician Corrie Hubert do a white-blood cell count and a thick blood slide. Reassured that this was malaria and not a bacterial infection, Jim gave the youngster some chloroquine as an anti-malarial and brought him home.

Soon afterward, David began vomiting, but the physician-father knew this was quite natural for a feverish child. Jim still didn't consider David's illness to be especially serious. So when fellow missionary Herb Foster stopped by, as planned, to go into the bush for a couple of hours of hunting, Jim at first hesitated, but then decided that it was safe for him to go. After all, he thought, Marilynn was a highly skilled nurse and, therefore, was perfectly suited to take care of their little son.

As it happened, however, Jim had been gone from Mukinge only twenty minutes when everything suddenly changed for the worse. David suddenly found it hard to breath. His color became ashen, then blue and almost black. Marilynn, cradling him in her arms, ran out to the car and drove the 150 feet to the hospital. She quickly slid out from behind the wheel and ran into the hospital, crying for suction.

On weekends, the hospital was run by student nurses, with one of the supervising R.N.s periodically making rounds. A newly arrived doctor, Dr. Bill Hicks, was on call. But he was temporarily living at the guest house on the other side of the hill. He would never have made it to the hospital in time to save David's life had it not been for God's providential timing.

Marilynn was surprised to be met at the door by Dr. Hicks and nurse Lill Brannon. Dr. Hicks had arrived by serendipity only a minute or two earlier. He had come over just to see if everything was running smoothly on the wards. (Jim believed that Dr. Hicks had been divinely summoned because he had no particular reason for being there.) And the young doctor would have been helpless without Nurse Brannon. Dr. Hicks was so new on the station that he didn't know where the equipment was kept—but Lill did.

Dr. Hicks tried suctioning David with an aspirating machine, but nothing could get through the little lad's airway blocked by his acute laryngospasm. Without any hesitation, Dr. Hicks grabbed a scalpel. David was so far gone that he didn't even flinch when the knife cut into his throat; by this time he had no discernible pulse. It was believed by all, including Marilynn, that he had died. She had held her baby boy all through the suctioning.

Then her fervent prayers were answered. After the tracheotomy tube was inserted and his airway was sucked out, David's color pinked up and his pulse was again discernible. The little limp body came back to life again.

A letter to the prayer partners back home, dated Sunday, August 9, 1959, vividly described David's status:

*David is still in critical condition. Marilynn and I were kept busy all through the night sucking him out at 10 to 15 minute intervals. There were many times of crisis when he was only a few minutes from death, but we are quite sure that he doesn't have brain damage since he is bright and alert when he is well sucked out. He has been taking fluids and jello well today and even worked up a smile for Terrie when she kissed him.*

*The Lord has provided here all the facilities needed to treat David—the electric aspirator, the electric croup kettles, the lab facilities. Even the drugs needed are available, and the tender loving care of the missionaries who are taking the load from us. Our hearts are overflowing with praise and adoration to the Lord for His perfect provision for us. Glory to God. Thanks so much for your faithful intercession.*

*All our love,*
*Jim and Marilynn*

It looked like the battle had been won. The next day, Monday, August 10, David was bright-eyed and perky. Jim was holding his son when big sister, Terrie, came in and started to rock in the rocking chair. The toddler struggled out of Jim's arms and walked over to the rocking chair. He rocked in it for over an hour, refusing all pleas to stop. The toddler gave each member of the family a big smile and a big hug. The prognosis looked good for a full recovery.

"We felt that he was definitely over the hump," Jim wrote in another letter dated Wednesday, August 12. "But late in the afternoon he went into a tailspin and started hyperventilating, then into severe bronchospasm . . ."

The telegram that followed was terse:

THE LORD CALLED LITTLE DAVID HOME LAST NIGHT. WE ASSUME HE HAD ACUTE TRACHEO-BRONCHITIS. A TRACHEOTOMY SALVAGED HIM FOR TWO DAYS, BUT HIS STRONG LITTLE BODY FINALLY TIRED, AND PNEUMONIA OVERWHELMED HIM. WE HAD EVERY DRUG AND INSTRUMENT NEEDED. IT WAS CLEARLY THE LORD'S PERFECT WILL. WE SORROW NOT AS THOSE WHO HAVE NO HOPE. RIVERS ARE NOT OVERFLOWING, BECAUSE HE IS WITH US AS WE PASS THROUGH THE WATERS. ISAIAH 43:1–2.

Jim and Marilynn then faced a decision that most bereaved parents never consider: Should they have a funeral?

Jim wrote in a letter:

*We have seen so much in the heathen "funerals" that remind us of parts of "Christian funerals" at home, that we weren't sure that we should honor his remains with a service. David was in heaven, and that was so real to us (and still is) that we could look at his casket with but little emotion, knowing that he is not in that box.*

But their African brothers and sisters in the Lord were used to showing emotion when a loved one died. The next morning, more than one hundred native women prayed outside the Foulkes house. They filed in fifteen and twenty at a time. They knelt by little David's crib, prayed aloud, sang several hymns, and then filed out. The women shuffled barefooted up the hall to the door, sobbing. Their tears were made even more precious to Jim and Marilynn

*The last picture taken of David.*

when they remembered that most of them had lost three or even four children.

The couple eventually decided to have a funeral in the church on the station. The pews were packed with Africans, some of whom had walked miles. Nearly all of the government officials from the boma attended the funeral. The Reverend Charles Foster wove the scriptural promises of eternal life, peace, and hope into his sermon. The message was even more poignant to those who knew that the Fosters themselves had lost an eighteen-month-old boy forty years ago, after moving to Northern Rhodesia.

Jim stood up during the service and told how he and Marilynn had placed David on God's altar when he was first lent to them. "We promised the Master that we would never interfere with His will for David's life. That commitment included death. And so, submitting to God's plan, gave us peace." The congregation then sang the moving children's hymn by Albert Midlane:

> There's a rest for little children above the bright blue sky,
> For those who love the savior and Abba, Father, cry;
> A rest from every turmoil, from sin and danger free,
> Where every little pilgrim will rest eternally;
>
> There's a home for little children above the bright blue sky;
> Where Jesus reigns in glory, a home of peace and joy;
> No home on earth is like it, nor can with it compare;
> For everyone is happy, nor could be happier there.

David's nearly three-year-old sister, Terrie, knew something big had happened, but she found it difficult to grasp the meaning of death. Everything seemed confusing. So many people were streaming in and out of the house. She felt a bit left out, watching the women closeted with "Mummy," praying in Terrie's and David's bedroom. No sooner had one group gone away then another was ushered in. Terrie was sure that after the first group left that it would be her turn. And, indeed, she was allowed to go in and sit on Marilynn's lap while wave after wave of praying groups continued to come in.

Terrie recalled years later, "I had such an ache after David was gone. During my nap time (when I wasn't sleeping), I'd look out our bedroom window into the blue sky. Somehow my heart found comfort in the blue of it, because it was heaven, and that's where David was. He'd gone to live with Jesus, I was told." She still had questions though.

"But will Jesus take as good care of David as we did?" she asked her parents. And when she was alone in her bedroom at night she would pray, "Dear Jesus, please send David down to play with me tomorrow."

The little coffin was carried around to the other side of Mukinge Hill and lowered into an unmarked grave alongside scores of other African children. The Africans were deeply moved by this ultimate act of identification. The local people had assumed that the young missionary couple would want their son buried in the European cemetary at the boma. The rumor had gotten around that they would take the remains to Ndola—a city three hundred miles away.

"It meant a lot to them that we laid the body right next to their own children," Jim wrote. "We didn't put a marker on the grave because we will never be going there again. David's immortality was so real to us that we felt the appropriateness of the words, 'Why seek ye the living among the dead? He is risen'" (Luke 24:5–6).

Jim and Marilynn's witness to the reality of Jesus' promise to Martha at the tomb of Lazarus—"I am the resurrection and the life" (John 11:25)—was used by God to win others to Christ.

The first fruit of this came only three hours after the service. The agricultural officer came to the Foulkes home with a beautiful bouquet of flowers from the boma officials. He told Jim that during the service, the Lord gave him faith to believe the gospel. He was gloriously converted. As soon as Marilynn entered the room, the agricultural officer told her the good news. Then he went over to the hospital to witness to the staff there.

The next morning, after hearing Jim tell of David's death and the victory over the grave that he and Marilynn experienced through their faith in the Lord, eight persons accepted Christ as their Savior in the outpatient department.

Jim recalled the profound effect that some of the local people had upon their grieving process. Amongst these was one Ba Kyabasanga, their nearest neighbor and a woman of faith whose own story had been marked by much sadness, but whose ultimate triumph through her reliance on God is worth telling in detail.

Kyabasanga had learned about Jesus when she was a girl of sixteen, working as a helper in the home of the C. S. Fosters around 1916. The Fosters were learning Kikaonde from Kyabasanga while she was learning about Jesus during the morning devotions. Those pioneer missionaries believed that the African teenager had been divinely selected, as they could not have known that this young, unsophisticated village girl had all the qualities needed to become a strong Christian leader.

Their daily teaching bore fruit; Kyabasanga gave her heart and life to the Lord Jesus Christ. A year or two after she had bowed her knee to Christ's lordship in her life, she married a young man named Joseph, another new believer. They established one of the first Christian homes in the entire district, vowing that they would always keep Christ at the center of their marriage. That vow would soon be tested.

All new brides in those days were expected to become pregnant, the sooner the better. Until that happened, the relatives on both sides of the family could not be satisfied that this was a good marriage. Three months after the wedding, Kyabasanga miscarried. The family saw the miscarriage as a clear sign from the spirit world that a taboo had been broken. To placate the offended spirit(s), it was necessary to offer a meal sacrifice and submit to the prescribed cleansing ceremony. Otherwise, the next pregnancy would also terminate in a miscarriage.

This was a major crisis for Kyabasanga and Joseph.

Would they, *could* they, really leave behind the ways of their forefathers? Strengthened by prayer, they became convinced that God would reward them and protect them for standing up against the wishes of their relatives and the generations-steeped tradition of their tribe. They knew their decision flew in the face of the worldview that they had been taught since early childhood.

How could they turn their backs on the accepted wisdom that all human events are controlled by the spirits of their ancestors who were even now hovering above the village ready to reward or to punish? The spirits had demonstrated their displeasure by causing a miscarriage. Failure to placate them invited further punishment. Almost certain barrenness or further miscarriages could be expected.

With all of these thoughts racing through their minds and the strong urging of their relatives to conform to tradition, they now had to make a decision. They made the right one.

Kyabasanga's and Joseph's decision was a momentous victory for the Kingdom of Light. They now had made a clean break with the old ways. They had joined Joshua in saying, "As for me and my house, we will serve the Lord" (Josh. 24:15).

This was not the end of the trial for the young couple. In fact, it was only the beginning. It became evident that Kyabasanga was a chronic aborter. After the third miscarriage, the entire village raged with anger at her when she again refused the cleansing ceremony. It was now obvious that the spirits of the village were aggrieved over the lack of sacrifice and ritual to atone for the miscarriages. It was also clear to the villagers that the spirits would punish the entire village for this sin.

Two children had died in the village since the couple's refusal to submit to the cleansing ceremony, making the villagers believe that the protection and good favor of the spirits had been withdrawn. There was nothing to do but to drive out the young couple so that a catastrophe could be averted. They were given a short time to pack their meager belongings, but the villagers made their banishment even more rapid by throwing rocks at them.

Then came a time of soul searching. What rewards had they gotten for putting their trust in Christ only? They had three miscarriages, had been cast out of their home, and were hated by their family. Was the creator God, *Shakapanga*, really more powerful than the ancestral spirits who had controlled the events of their forefathers for centuries? The Holy Spirit gave them assurance that "greater is He who is within you, than he who is within the world" (1 John 4:4).

Many years passed—years filled with pain and disappointment caused by further miscarriages. Each instance was a test of faith for the young Christian woman who was the first Kaonde to ever refuse the cleansing rites. But Kyabasanga never lost her belief that one day God would give her living children. That strong faith was finally rewarded when she delivered a healthy, full-term boy. His name? Yoba, the equivalent of Job in the local language. A daughter and a son followed after Yoba, and God received the glory.

The long period of difficult trials that Kyabasanga experienced served as the training ground for later leadership and exceptional service. She was a model for other Christian women because she had taken up her cross and followed Jesus. A respected leader wherever she went, her prayers in faith continually ascended to the throne of heaven.

Jim recalled, "I have always been thankful for Kyabasanga's ministry to our family. When our little son, David, died, she was our nearest neighbor and was the first to come and cry with us and to share the comfort with which she had been comforted. I thank God for every memory of Kyabasanga and Joseph."

A few months after David's death, the Foulkes family moved from the house where they were living when David had died. The McRuer family moved in, and Terrie would go and play with their two girls in the bedroom she and David had originally shared.

Terrie recalled:

Other times, I'd wander down the road that ran close to the old house. I'd look up at the sky which was really my sky, because it was David's Heaven Blue.

It was from the sky, in that direction, that something began to happen. I would first of all hear the beginning of a drone which got louder until a tiny speck appeared in the distance. The tiny speck got larger until it was revealed to be the most perfect, little blue plane, gracefully floating in and dropping down for a landing.

Somehow the blue of the plane, the blue of the sky, and even the blue of the pilot's eyes all mixed together with that same feeling of heaven in my heart. It was joy, exhilaration, and comfort.

# David

The miracle of it all is that forty years later, my sister Gwennie is married to the pilot's son. They live in our old house where David died. They have two little boys who sleep in David's and my bedroom, and those boys watch their father fly his plane from that direction of heaven.

Jim and Marilynn had been in Africa only one year when David died. The experience bonded them with the local people in a deep way that probably could not have happened otherwise. The support they received from the local Christians in their hour of need had given them a special love and sense of belonging—a relationship that helped them stay there for many more years. It also taught them they could trust the Lord completely, even if it meant walking through death's dark vale. They found that God's grace was indeed amazing. It was a grace they would have to rely on even more in the years ahead.

# ChapterTwelve
## A Home of Their Own

The grieving family also had plenty to occupy them on the domestic front. When the Foulkes family arrived at Mukinge Station in 1958, they were a family without a home. The South African General Mission (SAGM) had no building fund, so missionaries were expected to raise money from their supporters to pay for their homes. The goal, of course, was to keep building costs at rock bottom. (Jim always regarded the money given by supporters as coming from the Lord. And he treated it as such.)

But house construction is labor intensive. The good news was that labor was plentiful and cheap. The salary for a day laborer was a *ticky*—3 cents an hour or a quarter a day in terms of U.S. currency.

Marilynn drew up the plans for the house herself, so there was no need to pay for an architect.

Furthermore, the bricks used in the construction were free for the taking. All of the bricks were made out of a single giant ant hill in the front yard. (Anthills often get to be twenty feet high and can have a spike up to thirty feet.)

The bricks were made in the same way as they have been for thousands of years in various parts of the world. The red clay of the anthill was mixed with water and stirred until the slop had the consistency of thick porridge. Then the slop was poured into a wooden brick mold. The molded clay was placed in long lines in the sun in order to completely dry. For a semi-permanent dwelling, that was the end of the process. For permanent homes, however, the dried bricks were built into a massive kiln. The Foulkes's five-holer kiln was kept full of burning wood, night and day, until the bricks were completely fired. Fortunately, the hospital was surrounded by woods, making it easy to get the large amount of wood needed to keep the kiln fires burning.

Cement was so expensive in what was then Northern Rhodesia that cement mortar was only used on the first three courses of bricks. All the other courses were glued together with clay mortar. It may have been cheap but it had its drawbacks. White ants (termites) loved the clay; they would zigzag their way right up to the wooden rafters where they could chew away any soft wood.

Local hardwood trees that grew nearby were cut down by small axes handmade from auto springs. The felled trees were cut into logs of varying lengths, then dragged by a tractor to the mission's own sawmill where they were cut into boards and two-by-sixes to make rafters. Only the red, inner heartwood section of the massive trees, a type called ironwood, was used because it was resistant to the termites and the wood-bores that would eat up soft wood in short order.

Once seasoned, the board became so hard that a hole often had to be drilled to get a nail started, so the wood used had to be freshly sawed.

Obviously Jim and Marilynn couldn't oversee the work crew hired to construct their new home. (Alas, medical colleges don't offer courses in home building.) The Mukinge station's head handyman, Claire Gifford, supervised all of the construction. Claire grew up on a farm in the Canadian prairies, where when something broke or wouldn't work, you fixed it yourself. This Canadian farmer was multitasking before the word was even invented. "Claire was one of those guys who represented an essential element in keeping a mission operating," Jim said, admiringly. "In addition to supervising all of the building going on, Claire repaired the diesel engines of the truck and tractors on the station. It was also his job to keep the medical equipment at the hospital functioning around the clock. He always took time, however, for a spiritual ministry in the local church."

While waiting for their own home to be finished, the Foulkes family lived with other mission families. Dr. Bob and Belva Foster, who had four—eventually seven—children, were their first hosts.

# A Home of Their Own

*Pencil sketch of the Foulkes's house by Lori Hey. She served with her med-student husband, Lloyd, in 1988.*

Jim fondly recalled, "We were observant students for three months as we watched the dynamics of that home—the discipline, the love, the family devotions which included Bible verses and prayers from each of the kids daily around the dinner table. It was a model that we hoped to imitate in our own home."

Marilynn watched with intense interest how Belva prepared the local foodstuffs, knowing that soon she would have to run her own kitchen. Jim bird-dogged Dr. Bob through the hospital wards to learn the first stages of becoming a "bush doc." Jim was impressed by the evangelistic outreach of the hospital. Pastor Munguya, the hospital chaplain, tried to visit every patient every day. And all of the African senior staff were committed Christians.

Their next move was into the "luxurious home" belonging to Bob and Enid McRuer. Bob, the hospital pharmacist and administrator, and Enid, a doctor, were in Canada on furlough. "We enjoyed their comfortable, tastefully furnished house until they returned several months later," Jim recalled.

The house had been built by Enid's father, who had been a missionary in China until the Communist government took over. When he returned to Canada he had run a successful construction firm for many years. In his heart, however, he longed to be back on the mission field again. He offered his services to several mission organizations in Toronto. But short-term service for seventy-year-old volunteers was unheard of back then.

He finally knocked on the door of the SAGM Canadian director, who couldn't believe that here was a man offering to build houses for missionaries at his own expense! It was an offer he couldn't refuse. He was immediately sent to Northern Rhodesia (later to Angola), where he followed in the footsteps—spiritually as well as physically—of the Carpenter from Nazareth.

Dave and Elwanda Fields hosted the Foulkes family for the remaining months until their home was inhabitable. Dave was the mission/church liaison representative. Elwanda ran the outpatient department at the hospital. She also taught illiterate female church leaders how to read and write, and through Bible study, taught them how to progress from the milk to the meat of the Word. Marilynn would later have the opportunity to do a similar ministry among the women.

In the meantime, Dave was introducing Jim to the enchanting world of hunting in the safari country. Jim had always loved the sport of hunting. But in Africa it was more than a sport; the animals were killed to put fresh meat on the table.

On their first safari, Dave and Jim came upon a large herd of hartebeest. Their hunting licenses allowed each man two kills. By the time they had downed four of the beasts, David's powerful .30-06 rifle exploding near Jim's right ear had done serious damage. That experience, plus many other later hunting trips, would be partially responsible for Jim having to wear hearing aids. "No one, in those days in Africa, ever thought about wearing hearing protection," he said.

It took about one year from the time the land was cleared and the bricks were starting to be made before the Foulkes's new home was finished. The house still had to be painted and several doors still needed to be hung, but those minor matters were forgotten in the joyful excitement of moving into a brand new, fresh-smelling house that they could call their own. Before Christmas of that eventful year, they found themselves comfortably installed in the new home that they considered a gift from God.

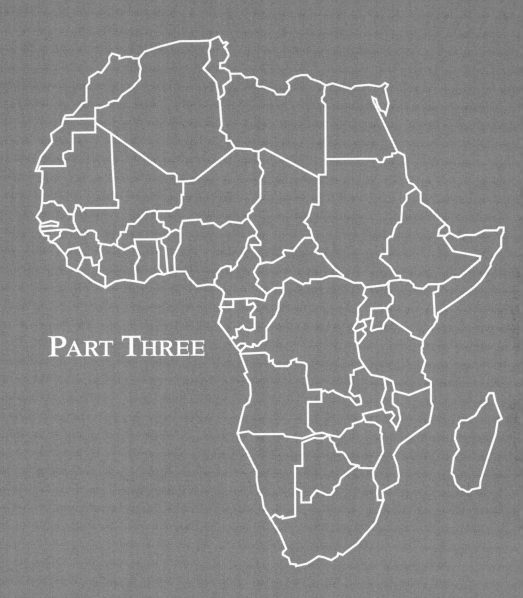

PART THREE

# ChapterThirteen
## Moving Adventures

An edition of the *Kaonde Hospital News* from 1962 describes the increasingly busy workload of the missionary staff due to expanding hospital facilities and the departure of Dr. Bob Foster to start a new hospital in the western province, south of Kasempa.

And so, the new medical superintendent of the Kaonde Hospital was Dr. Jim Foulkes. Alongside of him, Jim could rely on the medical talents of Drs. Bill Hicks and Enid McRuer and the half dozen missionary nurses, who functioned more like what we would nowadays call nurse practitioners. The workload and staff shortage were the main reason that Jim and Marilynn had to delay their furlough visit to the United States.

The Foulkes family returned for their first furlough in the middle of 1963. Jim's parents had been living in Lincoln, Nebraska, where Mr. Foulkes accepted an invitation from the *Back-to-the-Bible Broadcast* radio ministry to set up their donor program. It was decided that, since the furlough was scheduled to be for one year, the growing family would be based there in Lincoln, where Mother Foulkes had friends who owned a house.

The house was located in a rather rundown section of town, but it was spacious and inexpensive, and with supporters scattered across the continental U.S. and Canada, it turned out to be a conveniently located base for Jim's deputation trips.

And that space was needed, as the Foulkes family was entering a growth phase. Terrie now had two younger sisters, Gwennie (short for Gwendolyn) and Jill. Baby Jackie's arrival the following year delayed the family's return to Africa by several months. Terrie was soon to be the eldest of four Foulkes girls.

In Lincoln, she was enrolled in the second grade, making some friends among the local schoolgirls. This might have been

*Missionary staff, 1962. First row (left to right): Corrie Hubert, med tech; Ellen Groh, RN; Elwanda Fields, RN; Marilynn Foulkes, RN, BSCN; Eleanore Foster, RN; and Enid McRuer, MD. Back row (left to right): Bill Hicks, MD; Marjorie Harstine, RN, BSCN; Phyllis Spahr, RN, BSCN; Jim Foulkes, MD; and Bob McRuer, pharmacist.*

intimidating for her if she had not already spent a semester away at boarding school in Africa.

Missionaries in their part of Africa had few chances to provide their offspring with a good education. This was before the popularity of home schooling, and they were a long way from the nearest concentration of expatriates in Northern Rhodesia's Copper Belt. The only other alternative was to send their children home to the U.S. or England as some earlier missionaries had done. This was logistically and emotionally very difficult, not to mention quite beyond the family budget.

Jim and Marilynn chose to send their children to Sakeji School, located in the far northwestern corner of the country, close to the source of the mighty Zambezi River. That famous river gave its name to the newly independent country. (Northern Rhodesia changed its name to Zambia when the British handed over power to the local people in October 1964.)

The school was founded by Dr. Walter Fisher, reported to have been the first long-term medical doctor to arrive in the country. He arrived at the opening of the twentieth century as a pioneer missionary with Missions to Many Lands. Dr. Fisher chose the location of the school to be fairly close to his mission station at Kalene Hill in the area of the Lunda tribe.

The school was staffed by missionary teachers from the U.K. and North America, and had about a hundred students living on campus. The children slept in dormitories with rows of beds protected by mosquito nets. There was a noticeably English flavor to their education, a result of the school being started by Dr. Fisher when the country was still a British colony. Many of the teachers devoted their entire lives to Sakeji, and these ladies ended up being surrogate parents for several generations of missionary kids whose families, by necessity, sent them there to be educated.

Separation within the families was hard to bear, but the Foulkes family was no different from many other families who had to say good-bye to their little ones from the age of six onwards, not seeing them again for months. The mothers cried, the kids cried, and the fathers cried.

Marilynn would call the separation from the children "the hardest part of missionary service," and during a later home assignment, would comment that "one of the greatest blessings of furlough is the fact that I can kiss Terrie good-bye in the morning, put her on a school bus, and know that she will be home in the afternoon, rather than four months later."

One of the factors that made it a little easier from the child's perspective was the presence of their siblings at the school with them. The Foulkes children were there with the Foster children and other kids from Mukinge, as well as the children from missionaries working in other parts of Zambia, Southern Congo, and Angola.

The children shared many happy memories. It became an extended family system which helped sustain them through many a difficulty. A carpooling adventure illustrates this. In the wet season, Marilynn and "Uncle" Ginger Wright were driving to pick up a carload of Mukinge kids from Sakeji, with preschooler Jackie taken along for the ride. Parents were to pick up their respective pupils just after the Christmas program.

The day wore on, the program came and went, and the children waiting to be picked up by Uncle Ginger were disappointed when their ride did not appear along with all the others. It transpired that the lightweight van that Ginger had driven was not up to the challenge of the muddy, potholed roads. He had made very slow progress and, at one point, actually left the road and gently rolled over. What could a good Englishman say in such a situation except, "Would anyone like a spot of tea?"

They eventually made it and, not wanting to scare the Sakejiites for the return trip, the tired parents decided to stay mum about the accident part, until little Jackie innocently blurted out, "We fell over in Ginger's car!"

The adventure was not over, however, as the missionaries decided to take a different, possibly safer, route for the return journey home. All was well until the van was crossing a swollen river gorge. Coming out of the gorge, the van struggled up a steep grade, when halfway up the slippery slope, it lost all headway and began to roll ominously backwards toward the river.

At this point, Marilynn, in the back seat with several small fry and losing all confidence in the driver, wasted no time in opening the van's side door, grabbing the nearest child (a very surprised young Ken Foster) by the front pocket of his school blazer, and jumping out of the moving vehicle to safety.

*Daughter Terrie and her beloved Suzie. A snake bite while in the backyard almost ended Suzie's life.*

# Moving Adventures

As she sewed the pocket back onto the boy's blazer, the child's mother, Auntie Eli, thanked Marilynn for her prompt action to save her son, who had nevertheless stayed with the vehicle when the pocket left!

Except for Marilynn's sprained ankle, no harm came, as the van was soon restored to its forward progress—only after a large boulder at river's edge stopped the vehicle from plunging backwards into the roaring torrent. The trajectory of the out-of-control van had taken it wide of the bridge. It was a close call.

The vagaries of transport in Africa were often the source of some memorable situations. Wear and tear on the vehicles caused a rapid turnover. The Foulkes went through several Land Rovers and an International before the acquisition of their most famous vehicle, a Dodge truck nicknamed the "Big Orange," for its bright orange livery.

African "roads" could certainly take their toll. Travel in the wet season demanded four-wheel drive, a power winch, a bumper jack, several six-foot planks, plus an ax and shovel. In the dry season, the bumps and potholes played havoc with the suspension. For one vehicle, the tally for new shock absorbers was twenty-three!

Shortly after getting the Big Orange, Jim drove back from Sakeji, following closely behind a Smith and Youngson lorry. Jim was not renowned for his defensive driving. The way he put it to daughter Terrie: "I could never have a Christian bumper sticker on my car, because I often don't drive like one."

On this occasion, being close to the truck helped his visibility, since he was in the slipstream away from all the dust kicked up by the huge tires. All was well, apart from the usual bumpy ride for the passengers, until—for some reason—the lorry ahead came to an unheralded abrupt stop and the Big Orange sailed into its rear end.

Terrie remembers the silence as the engine died, followed by the inevitable tears of the jolted passengers. Ginger's wife, Dulcie, impaled her scalp on two screw tips that stuck down unprotected from the roof, bringing a torrent of blood down her face; Andy Fisher was thrown against a bird cage in the back, releasing the captive doves into the melee; and Terrie cried that their beautiful new truck was no longer pristine. The severely wounded truck had to be towed for the last fifty miles to Mukinge.

Terrie also remembers Jim spending hours on the dune buggy. In this project, he enlisted the help of maintenance engineer,

"Uncle" Len Aylett, who had all the mechanical skills that Jim lacked. Together, the two of them repaired, reassembled, tinkered with, and generally fussed over it for the better part of ten years. The most serious problem arose when the dune buggy broke into two pieces, requiring a major welding job by Uncle Len in the middle of the bush the next day.

Getting around in Africa was never more important than when the family went on picnics and weekend camping trips. Their extended family from the mission station, including the "Aunties," often went along for the ride. Game viewing in the nearby Kafue National Park and fishing in one of the Zambezi tributaries were favored venues; there were always lots of adventures.

The Foulkes girls all thought growing up in Africa was wonderful, apart from having to go away to boarding school.

# ChapterFourteen
## Daily Life in the Bush

E arly on, the Foulkes family experienced something of the culture shock that is common to most rookie missionaries. They initially depended for their social life on the close-knit group of fellow missionaries on the station and the few British officers nearby at the boma.

They lived 180 miles from the nearest grocery store and 120 miles from the nearest paved road. During the rainy season, the dirt roads turned to mud and were sometimes not passable, so everyone tried to lay in supplies for the several months when the road to town might be impenetrable.

The family soon developed a disciplined, routine way of living that reflected their priorities.

Jim would get up early to make his rounds at the *kip* (keep), short for *kipatela* (hospital in Kikaonde). Then there was the time of prayer and Bible reading with the hospital staff. When he returned home for breakfast, he always stomped the dust off of his shoes on each step leading to the walkway. The Foulkes children later remember that as the first signal that Daddy was home, and breakfast would soon follow. After entering the house, Jim would head for the bathroom to do his ritualistic scrubbing of his fore-arms and hands—as if "scrubbing in" for surgery. Actually, it was just the opposite—he was "scrubbing out" to cleanse himself from hospital diseases.

The weekday breakfasts never varied. The family's first cook, Kosita Kafumakachi, had been taught the art by a British doctor's wife in town. By the time Kosita became the Foulkes's cook, he was an older man, quite fixed in his ways. As a result, the family ate typical British fare daily.

Kosita came from a family of high achievers, but being the eldest son, he never had the opportunity to go to school, and as a result was illiterate. One of his brothers was the first Zambian to get a legal degree, another brother was the first Zambian to become a headmaster of a secondary school, and two of his other brothers were headmasters of upper primary schools. Sadly, Kosita never became a Christian, unlike the rest of his family. (He eventually had to be dismissed because of his repeated drunkenness.)

Kosita arrived every day at 6:00 A.M. to start a fire in the wood-burning kitchen stove. He would wash the last night's dishes, make porridge and toast, serve some in-season fruit, and set the table. Promptly at 7:00 A.M. he would ring the bell, summoning the family to the table.

Fruit trees grew in such abundance on the Foulkes property that it resembled a mini garden of Eden. There were mangoes, oranges, lemons, bananas, and mulberries—all for the picking. No forbidden fruit here. And on the mission station itself there were grapefruits, avocados, tangerines, and prickly pears.

Vegetables were also homegrown. With the help of their first "outside man," Petelo (and his successors), Marilynn became an expert gardener.

*An unusual baptismal scene. The hippo was raiding the hospital gardens night after night, so the district officer ordered Jim as an honorary game ranger to dispatch the raider. The dried meat fed the hospital inpatients for three months.*

# Daily Life in the Bush

"Gardening in a tropical climate is completely different from gardening in a temperate climate. The bugs were hungrier and the night feeding animals who frequented our plot were definitely a bigger problem than we had dreamed of," Jim explained.

The numerous game herds nearby provided all the fresh meat the family needed. The antelope species included impala, hartebeest, roan, sable, eland, kudu, waterbuck, and duiker. Warthog and buffalo added variety. Jim also hunted elephants (jumbos) and hippos, primarily to feed the hospital patients. Chickens also were raised for meat and eggs.

Jim and Marilynn were not above serving guests (without telling them in advance) jumbo, hippo, or even buffalo meat. "No reason to put them off before a tasty roast was already downed," he joked.

After breakfast, Jim would read a Bible passage with comments and then pray. Before going to work at the hospital, Marilynn had devotions with the household help consisting of the cook, the outside man, and the nanny. In one of her sessions, Marilynn told of Abraham, who was willing to sacrifice his only son to obey God. As the story says, an angel stayed Abraham's hand and God provided a ram to be Isaac's substitute. (There was no Old Testament in the Kikaonde language then.)

The story so gripped their cook Blackson (who succeeded Kosita), that he kept murmuring all day the phrase, "His own son, his own son." Blackson's life was changed the first time he heard the story. He saw the connection—and the difference—between the Abrahamic story and the death of God's only Son on the cross—a sacrifice that was not cut short by a substitute animal. Blackson spent the next week going around from campfire to campfire to share that wonderful story with his friends who had never heard it.

Jim and Marilynn arrived at Mukinge at a time when the missionary wives were expected to be involved "in the work" at least half a day if they had young children (otherwise, a full day). Marilynn's training as a nurse with a degree and good experience made her the best choice to be in charge of the outpatient department from 8:00 A.M. to 1:00 P.M.

The outpatient department was always crowded and noisy with lots of pushing and shoving in the long, unpatrolled waiting lines. Jim was convinced that the number of people crowding around Marilynn's desk contributed to her developing tubercular pleurisy.

That put her in the hospital for a month and it took three additional months for her to regain her strength. Some of the expatriate missionaries were more susceptible than others to the endemic parasitic diseases. During her first term of five years, Marilynn contracted malaria, bilharzia, hepatitis, and amoebiasis, in addition to TB and sleeping sickness.

Because of Marilynn's slow recovery from TB, Jim hired a bright eighteen-year-old local girl to live with them and help look after the children.

Jim said, "She was a seeker. She read the entire Bible during the first two weeks she was with us. And soon after became a devoted follower of Christ." Jim helped her get a scholarship to a secretarial school in London. She later became the private secretary to Zambia's first president, Kenneth Kaunda.

In the U.S., only well-to-do families have servants. Many would think it strange that a missionary family, living on the gifts of their supporters, would hire household help. But in the "ticky" economy, help is not only easily affordable, but good stewardship as well.

The African bush dwellers lived outside most of the time, using their grass-roof huts primarily as a place to sleep. Their diet generally consisted of thick, pasty *nshima* (corn mush) eaten out of a bowl or platter with their fingers twice a day. Only the lucky ones could get a job.

By employing servants, highly trained doctors and nurses could devote more of their time to the task for which they were trained and called—ministering to the sick and the injured. And the servants earned an income, some for the first time, that seemed to them like manna from heaven.

Take, for example, Petelo, who was wood chopper, drawer of water, and gardener in the early years. Petelo initially arrived at the hospital to get treatment for leprosy. When he was considered fully cured, he sought work. (Petelo always had a slight limp from his disability, as he walked on his permanently insensitive feet using protective sandals made out of car tires.)

Jim's supporters in his hometown of Lima, Ohio, had given him funds to buy an ambulance. But the gift had a catch—it turned out that the doctor had to be the ambulance driver. The second problem was that no one was able to pay for the long rides from the villages that might be eighty miles from the hospital.

# Daily Life in the Bush

*Pounding and sifting converts grain into a healthy flour that becomes mush, the staple food.*

One night, a distraught man arrived at the Foulkes's front door at 10:00 P.M., pleading that his wife was dying and needed to be brought to the hospital. After driving out seventy miles on the dusty, bumpy road, Jim and the husband arrived at the village of the dying woman.

Not only was she not dying, she even refused to get into the ambulance! By the time Jim had finished his Good Samaritan round trip, he had gotten only two hours of sleep. He made a quick decision: he would teach Petelo how to drive.

Jim started the driving lessons the next afternoon. A bright and hard-working young man, Petelo served as the driver until the ambulance wore out.

"I was able to get Petelo a good job with the government since anyone with a license could get a job as a driver in those early days," Jim stated.

It's all a matter of perspective: Jim's description of where they lived as at "the very end of the road" (some might say "the end of the world") differed from that of his growing young daughter. Terrie called it a "fairly major connecting road which ran in front of our house. All during breakfast and lunch we observed the world going by through our big picture window . . . women with loads of firewood on their heads, men with loads on their bikes, stray dogs. Uncle Len zooming past on his motorbike, forever smiling."

To Terrie, their dining room table "was a place of joy." They did indeed have a lot of guests—planned and unplanned. When Dr. Bob moved on, Jim became the hospital superintendent, so it was expected that guests would stay with the Foulkes. Some of the guests were VIPs—two months before he was elected president of the newly independent Zambia, Kenneth Kaunda stopped by with his wife to visit and have tea in the backyard. Sir Eric and Lady Mae Richardson spent several days in the Foulkes's home. Sir Eric was the chairman of the British arm of the mission. He had been knighted because of his founding of the largest polytech college in the world and for planting daughter colleges in the Third World.

Terrie recalled, spilling some of the family's early secrets:

One bone of contention in our house was that if visitors came to the hospital close to lunchtime, Daddy would invite them home for lunch. Sometimes he remembered to call home and warn Mummy, sometimes not.

I remember on more than one occasion looking out the window and saying, "Hey, who's that with Daddy?"

Mummy would say, "*Oh no!!!*" as we scrambled around to lay extra plates on the table and tried to stretch the lunch.

Our home was happy and energetic and open, part of the wider missionary station, who were our extended family. In later years, the Zambians became more of our community, as well.

Until 1972, a noisy generator supplied the electricity for the station. But diesel fuel was expensive, so the generator was used only during surgery and from 6:00 P.M. to 10:00 P.M. and on Monday and Thursday from 9:00 A.M. to noon so the families could do their laundry. The children used the morning hours of power to play records on their record player.

When extra hours were needed to read or get ready for bed, candles were used. Candles attracted so many flying insects, however, that it was scarcely worthwhile to try reading by one.

Under mosquito nets, flashlights were an option, but with batteries in short supply, they were a luxury.

When the generator was turned off, it suddenly became quiet, dark, and peaceful on the mission station. As Terrie recalled, "The gentle lights and sounds of the African night took over, like the sounds of drums beating in some distant villages."

The family's musical taste started out quite highbrow—undoubtedly due to Marilynn's classical background. But it gradually began to widen—or descend—depending on one's viewpoint. First came Bach, Leontyne Price, and Vivaldi. Then came the folk songs and singers—Pete Seeger; Peter, Paul, and Mary; followed by the Beatles.

Marilynn developed a love affair with Zambian harmony, syncopation, and differing rhythms, which never waned. She conducted choir practice in her living room for the nursing students, who particularly loved Negro spirituals. The church and youth choirs would sing indigenous songs, and some of the choir practices would go far into the night, singing praises to the King of Kings.

A young school teacher at Mukinge, Emmanuel Ezekiel, had been blessed with generous musical gifts. Marilynn taught him how to read music and play the piano. She hoped that Emmanuel would be the one to bring indigenous music to the churches.

*Marilynn leads the Mukinge choir in a hallelujah.*

Jim said, "He chose another path and really became the Elvis Presley of Zambia." Emmanuel became famous in Zambia, and he traveled and performed in other African countries and also Europe.

Two months before he died of kidney failure, Emmanuel stood up in one of the village churches and confessed his sins. "He wrote two hymns in those weeks before he died—a largely wasted life," Jim said sadly.

Emmanuel's popularity was enormous to the end—and after. When he died, the huge crowds that gathered to mourn him were too big to be handled in the capital city, so the decision was made to bury him at Mukinge where his roots were.

The vice president and a large entourage—including two or three of his wives—arrived in a huge army helicopter. The pressure from the helicopter's rotary blades lifted the roof off of the hospital's morgue.

"The governors, mayors, and members of Parliament who drove to the funeral emptied out the country's elite," Jim noted.

Marilynn would have to wait for many more years before the Lord selected another gifted Zambian who was faithful and who could compose and put Scripture and hymns into indigenous music.

Not all of Jim's missionary work was spent in the remote bush; he occasionally made it to the big city. On July 20, 1969, Jim arrived in Lusaka, the teeming capitol of Zambia, for an executive meeting of the Evangelical Church of Zambia. It was exciting enough that a television was in the mission guesthouse—there was none at the mission outpost—but a buzz was in the air this special day, and the TV served as a magnet for every person on the property. In thirty minutes, if all went as planned, a human being would set foot on the moon.

"I cracked open my new *Time* magazine as I waited for the historic moon shot," said Jim. The lead article gave details of the astronauts who were about to make history, including an Eagle Scout from Wapokaneta, Ohio.

"I smiled and looked up from my magazine, and I was sixteen again," recalled Jim. He, too, had been an Eagle Scout in Ohio, and had put forth the effort to have that eagle pinned proudly on his scout uniform.

Later, Jim directed waterfront activities at Shawnee Boy Scout camp in Ohio. One of his top waterfront assistants was a young lad who, when he turned sixteen, earned a pilot's license while most kids were content for just a driver's license.

Jim lowered his eyes again to the magazine article and locked onto the name of one of the astronauts. Jim recalled, "I let out a shout of recognition, 'That's my boy, Neil!'"

Within minutes, history unfolded and the broadcast of "one small step for man, one giant leap for mankind" was heard around the world—even in Zambia.

What a fantastic moment, "I felt that a little piece of me was with our 'extraterrestrial Columbus,' as Neil Alden Armstrong achieved that lofty walk amidst the stars," said Jim.

Years later, Jim was sitting around a blazing campfire, deep in the bush on the edge of the game park, with Benwa, his Zambian hunting buddy. Benwa was a man with an amazing memory. If he

*Benwa, Jim's hunting buddy. With his instinctive sense of direction, he always got them back to the mission station.*

heard the name of a river once, he never forgot it. He truly had a compass inside his head, as he claimed. Benwa would say, "I don't know any stars, I don't follow the landmarks, I just know where home is." He never once erred, even under pitch-black night skies in unfamiliar territory, to find the way home.

"I nodded toward the full moon and bragged to my friend in Kikaonde, the native language. 'Benwa, I know the man who walked on the moon.'"

Benwa laughed a long time, then glanced over at me and discovered that I was not joking. So Benwa just gazed into the fire, wondering what lunar fever had possessed his friend to say such a thing. He finally replied, "No one could ever walk on the moon! It is too far."

Jim realized that Benwa was quite serious in his disbelief. While the world press trumpeted the moon-shot heard 'round the world, scores of villagers had apparently been out of earshot.

"I am glad that Benwa did believe that the only begotten Son of God came to earth and lived a perfect life, and that He died to pay for the price of his sins, and that his faith in that act had reconciled him to God," said Jim. That is more than a lot of Westerners believe and infinitely more important than believing in a mortal man strolling on the moon.

"I say a resounding 'amen,' to astronaut James Irwin's conclusion that man walking on the moon was nothing compared with Jesus walking on the earth," stated Jim.

# ChapterFifteen
## Touching Leprosy

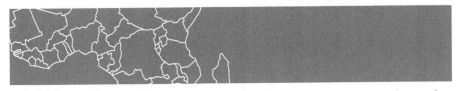

Jim was immersed in his work at the hospital where he continually met new challenges. One of the bigger challenges was treating leprosy patients at Mukinge. In Africa, those with leprosy were not considered untouchable as they were in India or had been in Palestine at the time of Christ. Even so, they were gathered into leprosaria as soon as they could no longer bring any benefit to their village. In Africa, as in many developing countries, leprosy was considered a dangerous, infectious disease: in fact, it is only very feebly infectious.

Leprosy is still one of the most feared diseases in the world. The stigma attached to persons with leprosy goes all the way back to biblical times. Historically, leprosy victims were required to be quarantined outside of the village, and if anyone came close to them, they were required to shout out loudly, "Unclean! Unclean!"

In the Middle Ages, those diagnosed as having leprosy were kept isolated in leper houses for life. They were considered legally dead and deprived of any property. Meanwhile, their spouses could remarry with the blessing of the Church. The inhabitants of the leper houses in the Middle Ages were almost all cruelly misdiagnosed, since leprosy is a tropical disease and extremely rare in Europe.

Jim recalled that in recent years, a woman in the U.S. was referred to Carville, formerly the National Leprosy Center in Louisiana, for a skin biopsy that her doctor thought might represent leprosy. When the biopsy report came back, the woman expressed her relief by exclaiming, "Thank God, it's only cancer!"

In the Gospel of Luke, written by the beloved physician, we find the statement, "Jesus reached out his hand and touched the man" who suffered from leprosy. Jesus broke a taboo with His healing touch to make a man well.

*A Sunday school class for the children in the leprosy colony. The student nurse helped Marilynn teach the class. The colony closed down in the 1980s, since multi-drug prescriptions cut down the incidence of leprosy.*

In much of the world, leprosy was considered an untouchable disease. For centuries, the only people who would touch them were believers who followed in the footsteps of the Lord Jesus. In fact, when Jim first arrived in Northern Rhodesia, the Ministry of Health operated just one small unit for leprosy patients. All of the other thousands of leprosy sufferers were cared for by mission hospitals. Millions of dollars were raised by the American Leprosy Mission and the British Leprosy Mission for the care of patients around the world.

Jim noted, "That generous support came from Christians. The great pioneers in leprosy care were men like Robert Cochrane, Professor George Stanley Browne, and Paul Brand. All were medical missionaries early in their brilliant careers." (Jim attended lectures by Professor Browne in London for a week, and by Dr. Brand at Carville during two of his early furloughs.)

Dr. Brand had a profound effect on Jim, and is well known to a wider, non-medical audience through the several books he wrote, particularly *In His Image* (Zondervan, 1981) and *Fearfully and Wonderfully Made* (Zondervan, 1984), coauthored with Philip Yancey.

*A glorious day in June 1955, when Marilynn and Jim spoke their vows before God, family, and friends in Toledo, Ohio.*

*Mukinge Hospital in 1962 (there was no other hospital within 150 miles).*

*Dinner assured for several months.*

*Gwen with pet duiker.*

*Terrie and David.*

*Preaching in outpatient compound, 1960.*

*Missionary children often have exotic pets. Senior game guard Kyanamina was making rounds and walked too close to a hidden lioness. The protective instincts of the lioness required her to attack Kyanamina and he had to shoot her to save his life. Her three lion cubs were bottle fed by Ely Foster, so her children, David, Stanley, and Janet, had some adorable cuddlies to play with. One of these cubs later was in the movie* Cleopatra *and the other two were featured in the book and movie* Return to the Wild.

*The entire family attended Terrie's graduation from Rift Valley Academy in Kenya. RVA provided an excellent high school education, but being separated for three months at a time was very hard on all.*

*When the missionary kids returned home from boarding school, there were always jobs awaiting them, as well as a special family holiday.*

*The joy of the African bush. This photo was taken by Dr. Dick Furman shortly before Jim required three shots to down an animal. In jest, Dick commended him for his sportsmanship in firing two warning shots.*

*The Foulkes boys in 1982, with their eighty-nine-year-old mother (who would live another eighteen years).*

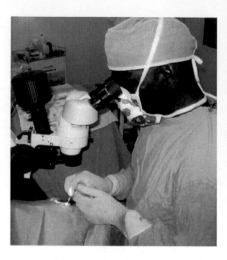

*Jairos Fumpa, special friend and assistant, now a fully certified eye surgeon.*

*Jim Adams, dear friend and supporter from OSU days, who also revised Jim's rough manuscript for this book.*

*Graduation is a joyous celebration. The principal tutor pins on the badge and gives the diploma to the happy graduate.*

*The happy couple, Jim and Martha, on their wedding day in 1979.*

*What a joy to have worked with these godly men who served as senior church leaders: David Mukimwa, Bishop Sam Kasonso, Pastor Kayamba, Pastor Kyomakyoma, Deputy Bishop Enos Masuhwa (later bishop), and Steve Weiandt.*

*Home assignment, 1982. Terrie, Jim, Martha, Gwen, and Jackie.*

*Dr. Richard Furman and his wife, Harriet, at Victoria Falls, after serving at Mukinge.*

*Franklin Graham presenting the 1998 Award for Excellence in Medical Missions to Jim at the World Medical Mission's Prescription for Renewal.*

*Joe Lacy persuaded Jim to write out some of his adventures. He and his wife, Winkie, then expertly put those disconnected yarns into book form. Their son Coleman is on Winkie's lap, and Bennett is on Joe's lap.*

Yancey originally teamed up with Dr. Brand to write a book that stressed the value of pain and disappointment in the Christian's life, but ironically, one of the major problems with persons with leprosy is their lack of pain. When the leprosy bacillus invades nerve tissue such as the corneal nerve, it deprives the window of the eye from a painful warning of dust, an insect, or any foreign body which might injure the eye. One injury follows another to the unprotected cornea, and often the final outcome is blindness from severe scarring.

Similarly, the feet and hands, deprived of the protective function of pain, are at the mercy of hot objects such as a cigarette, which can burn right down to cook the unfeeling flesh. Thorns, sharp stones, and ill-fitting shoes can do terrible damage to insensitive feet. Loss of digits and often amputation are the result of repeated injury and infection. "It goes against the grain of conventional wisdom, but the fact is that pain is good—even essential," Jim emphasized.

"This truth is a clear dividing line between biblical truth and the wisdom of the world system which says you should avoid pain at all costs," Jim said, a note of urgency in his voice. (He had preached a lot of sermons on the subject.)

"Disappointment, sickness, and emotional pain are part of the universal human experience. The Christian understanding is that with God's help, this suffering can be accepted and even beneficial. Paul's word of encouragement to the persecuted church in Corinth was: '. . . For our light and momentary troubles are achieving for us an eternal glory that far outweighs all' (2 Cor. 4:17). The fact that there is a design and purpose in suffering for a Christian is an understanding that separates the believer from the worldview of the non-Christian."

So what's the nature of this disease? What's at the bottom of the infection?

The leprosy bacillus, a first cousin of the TB bacillus, shares in the distinction of being a chronic, slow-growing bacterial invader. The bacteria multiply slowly in the body of those infected and require very long treatment. Fortunately, leprosy is only mildly infectious. It takes extensive exposure to one who is infected with living bacilli in order for the disease to be passed to another person.

Jim explained, "Even though as care providers we regularly touched our patients while examining them and treating them, we didn't worry about contracting leprosy since our contact was so short."

The distinctive feature of the leprosy bacillus is that it lives and multiplies in the tissues of the skin and nerves. Nerve involvement causes tingling first, then partial numbness, and finally anesthesia.

Jim observed, "It's easy to ignore early skin lesions and tingling, but those symptoms represent the golden months before irreversible deformities start to appear. It was always sad to receive new patients in the 1960s and 1970s whose bodies already looked like a battlefield."

Too often, persons with leprosy would not go for treatment until they were literally chased out of their villages because they were considered worthless. Generally, their spouses would reject them at an early stage. Often, the leprous person would eventually be unable to hold a hoe or an ax with his clawed, insensitive hands that were severely deformed and scarred from repeated burns. The feet would typically be severely damaged as well.

Joy Warner, a physiotherapist, and the daughter of an Anglican vicar, came on staff in 1965. She spent most of her time rehabilitating leprosy patients. Joy was also trained in prosthetics and worked wonders fitting the amputees with artificial limbs. Her shoe shop made specially padded sandals with microcellular rubber that protected their insensitive feet from ulceration. Every week, more than a hundred inpatients in the leprosarium gathered to get their medicine, and every hand and foot was carefully examined by Joy for early detection of skin deterioration. She was tireless, indeed a "joy" to all the patients she helped in this important ministry.

As in so many other areas, it's the ministers themselves who end up being ministered to, as much as their clients. Jim recalled:

> The response of the untouchable to the touch of love was beautiful to see. Some of the most earnest, fully devoted followers of Jesus Christ that I have ever known are pitifully deformed—but are beautiful in the eyes of God.
>
> I will never forget the testimony of one man as he stood on his peg leg and raised two useless hands heavenward and thanked God for allowing him to contract leprosy so that he might come to the leprosarium and find new life in Christ.

Joy's contribution was enhanced by an important addition to the leprosy team, Dr. Ray Foster. He was an orthopedic surgeon who had received lengthy training in India, where he learned special surgical corrections for leprosy sufferers. Dr. Foster flew his own plane to Mukinge three or four times a year. He would spend a week repairing clawed hands (using Dr. Brand's procedure) and did corrective surgery on dropped feet and paralyzed eyelids.

"Ray was considered a flying angel by the many who benefitted from his skill," Jim said.

An elderly village woman named Kyapabaya was a living example of how one could be horribly deformed by leprosy and still find victory in Jesus. This

*This leprosy patient was late in arriving for help, and had lost his forefoot and had moderate clawing of his hands. Intelligent and energetic, he eventually became the hospital cobbler.*

saintly woman had lost both legs, amputated below the knees (again, largely because she delayed going to the hospital until after her feet were virtually destroyed by repeated ulcers and infection). The hand she waved in a warm welcome to anyone approaching her hut was missing several fingers and was severely clawed. Her smile was beautiful even though much of her face was frozen in the leonine facies (face of a lion) of lepromatous leprosy.

The author had the privilege of meeting her one Sunday.

After church we streamed outside, and I was introduced to Kyapabaya, a disheveled woman kneeling by her cooking fire. She pointed the stub of her hand at several modest rows of corn. "Look at my field." The field was green, undisturbed. "God provides for me." She spoke again as if she wasn't understood. "Look! God provides for me. He does not allow birds to land on my field."

The field adjacent to Kyapabaya was peppered with marauding black and white magpies, squawking and flapping in and out of the corn rows. But, as if an unseen shield was present, no bird landed on her small patch.

Though Kyapabaya could not walk, she had found a way to stand above her circumstances with a heart of gratitude for God's provision. Pain in life may be inevitable, but succumbing to misery is optional. My encounter with the disabled woman was brief. The profound lesson she taught me about thanksgiving and faith, however, will stay with me the rest of my life.

Prior to 1950, the drug treatment of leprosy was a long history of failed attempts. Chalmoogra oil was almost universally used, and its "success was right on a par with the incantations of the witch doctors," Jim remarked. A dramatic breakthrough was made in the early '50s with the discovery of sulfone, a sulfa derivative, at Carville.

The early euphoria of the "end of leprosy" was soon tempered, however, by the drug resistance that occurred in the '60s. Finally, though, the introduction of multi-drug therapy by the World Health Organization in the mid–'80s resulted in dramatic rates of cure for old cases and allowed for comparatively short outpatient care for new cases.

*Auntie Joy Warner and Auntie Ness Aylett dressing wounds at the leprosy village.*

*Partial hospital staff with visiting dignitaries, 1965. From left: Joy Warner, physical therapist; Phyllis Spahr, RN, BSc matron/tutor; Alex Henderson, MD; Doraine Ross, RN; the author; Marilynn Foulkes, RN, BSc; Matiya Lotala, lab (behind Marilynn); Maluben Kashale, pharmacy; Peter Matoka, honorary minister; Nachi Kamukwamba, medical assistant (behind Peter); unidentified gentleman; Kennedy Mukimwa, lab; the provincial commissioner; Hilda Dube Zen, RN; and Joshua Munkena, X-ray tech.*

Jim declared in a triumphant tone, "This has been one of the greatest success stories of any tropical disease. The day of millions of people living in leprosaria in the tropics is over. The history of the care of leprosy sufferers is one of which Christians can be proud."

In the late 1970s, the Ministry of Health ordered that all "burned-out" (those without living bacteria but still left with deformities as a result of active disease in the past) leprosy cases be discharged from the various leprosy settlements throughout Zambia to their home villages. That presented a problem to some of the patients in Mukinge's leprosarium, Shikata, since they had lived there for twenty years. Many of them had no homes and were still severely disabled. They were not infected by living leprosy bacteria, but they still suffered from the permanent deformities that had occurred when they were actively infected.

For those who couldn't return to their home villages, the hospital started a half-way house where they could be given needed care.

By the Ministry of Health order, the government unwittingly scattered a veritable diaspora of mature, well-taught Christians far and wide to villages where there was no previous witness. Many new churches were formed. "The scattering had a most positive effect on the work of the Kingdom," Jim said.

There were 150 inpatients living in Mukinge's leprosarium when Jim arrived. When he retired in 1997, the hospital was only diagnosing four or five cases a year, and they were all treated as outpatients.

What a victory! The compassionate example of Jesus challenged His followers to reach out in a special way to this group of people who were often totally neglected by their governments and ostracized by their own families. It was Jesus Himself who gave these outcasts new hope and new life. To Him be the glory.

# ChapterSixteen
## Jumbo Hunter . . . or Hunted?

T he tsetse fly, which carries in its red-hot, needle bite the lethal African sleeping sickness, was indirectly the reason Jim and his pastor-partner, Ba Kalima, went hunting for an African bull elephant to fill the hospital's massive freezer. Because of sleeping sickness, the nearest cow was more than a hundred miles away.

The absence of beef cattle posed an ongoing challenge in obtaining fresh meat for the hospital's inpatients. The only way to provide the needed meat was to hunt the wild game that was plentiful nearby.

Jim explained, "One of the unwritten job descriptions for a doc at Mukinge was the requirement that he provide meat for the 160 inpatients (later 200) with his rifle. That meant he had to shoot a big animal at least once a year to provide the protein-rich meat that was served once a week." And no animal quite filled the bill—or the freezer—like a huge bull elephant.

At that time, Kasempa District alone was home to more than ten thousand elephants. (Poachers had not yet decimated the ranks of these national treasures to supply the ivory market.) Zambia's Kafue National Park is one of the largest in the world, covering territory the size of Wales. In addition to elephants, its diverse habitat shelters countless antelope, huge herds of Cape buffalo, and all the big cats.

It was a crisp, clear morning midway through the dry season when Jim and Ba Kalima began their hunt for big game near the border of the Kafue park. They had often hunted together through the years and had developed a respect for each other's skills.

"My only skill was pulling the trigger of my .458 rifle, and Kalima's was everything else," said Jim, chuckling. The confidence that the two men had in each other was most vital in hunting dangerous game.

Ba Kalima, pastor of the Mukinge Church, was an expert tracker and a master of bush survival. He knew the berries you could eat and the time of year when certain fruit from trees was edible. His ability to look at a bruised piece of grass sticking up in rock-hard ground in the dry season and be able to tell if an elephant had stepped on it, and if it was thirty minutes or three hours ago, continued to amaze Jim.

Beyond Kalima's extraordinary skill as a naturalist and tracker, the pastor was greatly respected as a man of godly wisdom. He also served as the church district superintendent, caring for sixty churches in the Kasempa District. As the missionary liaison for three years, Jim had to visit all sixty churches during the year. Pastor Kalima would always accompany him.

Jim remembered, "Every morning before the sun came up, he would pray out loud like all of our church people did."

But it was Jim who prayed out loud as he and Pastor Kalima looked like they were about to be trampled to death by twenty-six enraged elephants. It happened like this:

Kalima and Jim were thirty-five miles from the hospital, close to the border of the Kafue National Park. The African elephants they were hunting are amazing animals. They can be heard at great distances crashing through the bush, yet they can also move with unbelievable stealth, sometimes so silently that the only way to know they are hidden in the foliage is the loud rumble of gas in their intestines.

The men came to a huge open plain where, in the middle of the vast expanse, there was a herd of twenty-six elephants, more than half a mile from the tree line. The grass on the plain had been burned off, denying the two hunters of any cover between the tree line and the grazing jumbos.

A huge bull stood in the middle of the herd, his back a full two feet higher than the others. Four or five young ones were milling

*The main entrance into the northern sector of Kafue National Park required Jim's "go any-where" dune buggy during the rainy season. With thirteen inches of rubber on the road, the only time it got stuck was in the middle of a swamp. Martha and the Byers had no worry about safely crossing this thirty-foot stretch of water.*

around the herd. The protective instincts of the mothers and the "aunties" are so highly developed that the slightest whiff of human scent would send them on a deadly rampage to wipe out the trespassers.

Jim and Kalima were keenly aware that their lives were at risk in the kind of situation in which they had placed themselves. Man is the only true enemy of the five-ton elephant. As a bush surgeon, Jim conducted a number of postmortems on villagers and hunters

*Pastor Kalima, a dear friend and hunting partner.*

killed by lions, leopards, Cape buffalo—and elephants.

Jim's mind harked back to the memorable day that the police arrived to set up a postmortem time. Jim decided to do the postmortem immediately, but when he arrived at the morgue, he saw no sign of the cadaver. Mystified, Jim asked for the location of the body. The officer pointed to a gunny sack that he was carrying. Inside there were a few ghastly bits and pieces that looked like body parts. Jim protested that he did not do postmortems on fragments of human extremities.

"Let me explain," the officer said. He then told of a man in the community who had poached an elephant close to the village. It was getting dark and he scurried back to recruit some helpers to cut up the animal. The men in the village had been sitting around drinking beer all afternoon and had become quite drunk. But they rushed out as best they could to help their friend, envisioning a large supply of meat as their reward.

When they got back to the site of the "dead" elephant, they found the huge beast had regained consciousness and vanished. Scattering out in a frenzied hunt, one unlucky man found the wounded elephant. He quickly lifted his muzzle loader to fire—too late.

The jumbo grabbed him with his trunk, making a human baseball bat out of him by smashing him repeatedly against a tree. The elephant then completed his revenge by disarticulating the man and scattering his remains over a quarter of a mile.

"All that could be recovered were these bits of body parts," said the officer, nodding toward the gunny sack.

That memory of an elephant's fury seemed pertinent to the present situation since Jim and Kalima were out in the open without a blade of grass to hide behind.

Because of severe myopia, the African elephants don't depend on their eyes to detect potential enemies unless there is considerable movement. Elephants don't have to depend on their hazy eyesight because their extremely acute hearing and heightened sense of smell are so formidable. It is generally believed that an elephant can smell water a mile away.

Following a serious discussion of the dangers involved in getting close enough to kill an elephant, as opposed to the possible reward of tons of meat, Jim and Kalima made a tough call.

"The big bull was a five tonner, and that was enough to push us into the calculated danger. We needed the meat and the decision was to go after it," Jim recalled, matter of factly. No professional hunter would ever dream of guiding a client into such a dangerous situation, since "A dead client is bad for business," Jim joked.

To get within shooting range of the elephants without being spotted or smelt, Jim and Kalima adopted the army creep-and-crawl technique. They had to crawl inch by painful inch on their bellies, propelled by their bent elbows, over the black grass stubble to close the distance between them and their deadly prey.

Every minute or two, Jim stopped and shook out a tiny bit of flour from an empty cartridge to make sure that the wind was either dead still or blowing toward them—a sudden change in the wind could doom them.

The men snaked along on their bellies until they were a hundred yards from the herd. "At that point, you begin to wonder what in the world you are doing there. If you can still muster up enough saliva to lick a postage stamp, you are definitely overconfident," Jim recalled.

They were still not close enough, however, to get a humane pinpoint shot to the brain, so the two men worked up the willpower to drag themselves to within the required fifty yard range.

Finally, the bull presented a full side-view of his massive head. Jim, a crack shot, aimed his rifle. He knew that the steel-jacketed bullet had to enter a precise point one-third of the way from the ear hole to the eye. He held his breath and squeezed off a shot.

# Jumbo Hunter . . . or Hunted?

The mammoth bull dropped with a tremendous thud, and Jim heaved a sigh of relief. He knew that even an inch off the mark could mean the difference between a clean kill, or just giving the elephant a bad headache and a bad temper.

But after only about four minutes, the big bull staggered to his feet like a punch-drunk boxer—having only been knocked unconscious. At that moment, Jim and Kalima experienced something akin to unadulterated terror. With the wounded bull bellowing out fierce protests, absolute bedlam broke out. The entire herd, inflamed and madly trumpeting, stomped their feet, kicking up a dust storm that swirled twenty feet above their heads. Trunks were up in unison sampling the air, all focused on one question: Where is the enemy?

The elephants readied for a concerted charge; they would stop at nothing to destroy their enemy. Jim and Kalima could do nothing but shake uncontrollably at such a demonstration of fury and power.

It got worse.

The five other helpers in the hunting party were huddled at the tree line. Frightened by the boiling agitation of the herd, they bolted, trying to put as much distance as possible between themselves and the revenge-seeking elephants. Despite their poor eyesight, the elephants picked up the movement of the fleeing men and formed a solid phalanx, charging at top speed.

Lying flat on their stomachs, Jim and Kalima were instantly aware that they were in the direct path of seventy tons of jumbos as they stormed toward the fleeing men at the tree line.

Jim said:

We knew we were dead, but our survival instincts forced us up and running in a futile dash, knowing full well that even the fastest sprinter had no chance of outrunning an elephant.

But rather than getting trampled to death lying down, it seemed better to run and extend our lives a few extra seconds.

The first glance over his shoulder shocked Jim—the herd had already halved the men's lead. Jim had already left the old pastor behind. His comment was, "for whatever distance I ran with that trumpeting herd pushing me along, I might well have shattered a world record." If they had been chased by a lone bull, the guy who pulls ahead earns a ticket for another hunt, since the one elephant would stop and concentrate on one victim. In this case it would have only bought a split second. A second look didn't require much turning of the head, as the herd was just ready to run them down.

Jim related, "With the ground shudder racing up our legs, my prayer at that moment is just as vivid now as it was then." As his life flashed before his mind's eye, Jim heard himself cry out: *"Lord, I'm coming home!"*

At that precise moment, the miracle happened.

The thundering herd, only a few steps behind Jim and Kalima, its trumpeting blaring at ear-splitting decibels, suddenly executed a sharp right-angled turn. It was almost as if by command.

For the next ten minutes, Jim and Kalima listened to the herd crashing through the dense forest off to their right, stomping on bush and tree, still screaming as it raced farther and farther away.

Jim and Kalima didn't stop or even slow down as the herd disappeared in the distance. No, they just kept on running, as fast as they could, headed for the distant tree line. As soon as Jim's tortured breathing slowed down enough to be able to talk, he looked at Pastor Kalima and asked, "What happened?"

The old pastor, catching his breath, simply stated with no hesitation: "Man disobeys God, but animals never do. When God speaks, they listen. The Lord told them to turn right and they did."

Down through the years, Jim has never doubted that the explanation given by Pastor Kalima was the right one.

Jim says:

Being saved from imminent death magnified our trust in God for our earthly lives as well as eternal lives. That nerve-wracking experience made it even clearer to us that the Lord is ultimately in control of the events of heaven and earth. I thank Him for the miraculous extension He granted our lives that day.

Some twenty years later, at the funeral of Pastor Kalima, Jim had the opportunity to give a brief account of the elephant story. "In concert, we gave thanks to the all-powerful God who extended our beloved Pastor Kalima's life and ministry for two more decades, by issuing a command to a herd of angry elephants that they could not disobey. Pastor Kalima preached the remainder of his life on the importance of listening to God—like the elephants."

# Chapter **Seventeen**
## Danger in the Bush

T he elephant is only one of the many dangerous wild animals in Zambia that grudgingly share their habitat with human beings. High on the list of killers are lions, leopards, hippopotamuses, crocodiles, and a variety of poisonous snakes. Jim had close brushes with several of the above animals, and has treated victims of all of them.

"In the African bush, it is always wise to be prayed up, since opportunities abound to depart for the next life on short notice," Jim said, only half jokingly.

While riding with legendary game ranger Rolly Morris, Jim was once given a short-notice invitation by a rogue lion. The ranger had received reports of two old male lions killing village dogs and terrorizing the villagers.

Lions normally do not care for the flavor of human flesh. It is quite unusual for a pride of lions to switch menus and begin to hunt humans as a source of food. Man-hunting lions are usually old male lions who have been driven out from the pride by younger, stronger males. These retired oldsters often hunt as a team, since they can no longer benefit from meals provided by the highly efficient predatory machine of the pride's entire female population, which normally provides fresh meat for the king of the beasts.

As in humans, the teeth of old lions deteriorate with age. A broken fang can prevent them from sinking their teeth deeply into the necks of their prey, hindering the strangling maneuver which is the lion's common way of killing. Thus, the old-timers are reduced to killing village dogs, which are much easier prey than wild animals.

The next step down this ladder is for a lion to hunt humans. To descend to these depths, the lion would have to be really hungry. Once the lion gets the taste of human flesh, however, he wants more. He quickly learns that an unarmed man is a much easier quarry than chasing down a Cape buffalo, which might gore him to death, or a fleet-footed zebra that might kick him silly.

Jim and Rolly were together one weekend in the bush where the rogue dog-killers had been reported. They soon spotted two old male lions that fit the description of the outlaw cats. Ranger Rolly dropped one with a clean chest shot. The other lion bolted, running at top speed, then disappeared behind a huge twenty-foot-high anthill.

Jim and Rolly were sure the runaway lion was trying to put as much distance as he could between himself and them. They blithely barreled along in hot pursuit, riding in the open Land Rover with no windshield and no top.

They were within thirty feet of the anthill when the lion suddenly emerged with a booming, blood-curdling roar. Jim had been told by many old native hunters that if given a choice between a lion or a buffalo, they would prefer the buffalo. An old hunter offered, "The buffalo gets on with the business and does it quickly; the lion kills you twice—before he starts his job (by his fearful roar) and after he has got you at his mercy."

"The volume of that close-up roar and the terror of seeing that six-hundred-pound animal poised to pounce onto our heads made me freeze," Jim admitted.

Before Jim could recover and get his rifle up to his shoulder, the cool and calm ranger slammed on the brakes, grabbed his .30-06 rifle, and fired a round right into the beast's heart.

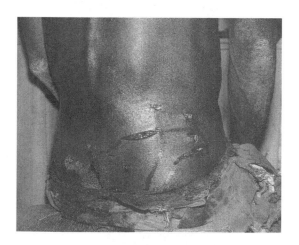

*This patient's shirt was no protection for the lion's paw that raked his back and threw him to the ground.*

# Danger in the Bush

"A good thirty minutes passed before my adrenaline level ratcheted down to normal again," Jim said with admiration in his voice for Ranger Rolly.

As predicted, the teeth of the old lions were badly worn down. One canine was missing entirely, making it nearly impossible to capture and kill wild game.

The two dead lions were laid out in Jim's front yard, attracting a crowd of several hundred people. As they skinned them out, the villagers were invited to take as much meat as they wished. None partook, though, because of a strict taboo against eating cats.

That experience allowed Jim to appreciate in a new way the serious warning by the apostle Peter that the "devil walks around like a roaring lion, seeking whom he may devour" (1 Pet. 5:8).

One day, some game guards from the Kafue National Park brought in the mangled body of a woman for Jim to perform a postmortem exam. The pug marks (paw prints) all around the site of the kill confirmed that she had been attacked by a pride of lions.

"There wasn't much left to examine," Jim recalled sadly.

It only took a few days for the local interpretation of the terrible event to become widespread. The woman reportedly had abandoned her husband in Luampa, one hundred miles away, and was running away to the Kasempa District, where she had relatives.

Her angry husband reportedly went to a local witch doctor and purchased a death sentence on his wife. The rumor was that the shaman had conjured up a magic lion that had done the will of the aggrieved husband by punishing his wife with a terrible death.

This explanation seemed to satisfy most people. Normally lions would not kill people, but according to folklore, supernatural lions break the rule.

"This interpretation brought terror to the entire district, and it became the main topic of conversation," Jim said.

And then it happened again.

Four lions attacked a village close to the game park while the people were huddled around an evening campfire. The men all had spears because they were on high alert since the previous attack was on the road, close to their village.

Without warning, the lions sprang on them from out of nowhere. One man was killed instantly and two more were badly wounded before the other men were able to kill one of the lions and drive the other three off.

It took a long time to get the message from the village to the police sixty miles away, and for them to obtain a vehicle and fuel for the trip to the hospital. So it was in the middle of the next night when Jim got a call from the hospital watchman, summoning him to take care of the two badly mauled men.

Jim recounted, "When I got to the hospital, I could see by my flashlight that the police had dumped a huge lion right at the entrance, with the dead man sprawled next to him. I never did understand why the lion was deposited with me, since I had no intention of doing a postmortem on a lion!"

"But the situation was without precedent and the police obviously weren't sure what to do with the dead cat," he said.

The two men mauled by the lions were in critical condition. Both had lost a lot of blood over the twenty-four-hour period since they had been attacked. One lion had run its large paw down one man's back from his neck to his buttock. The long claws severed tendon and muscle alike, not stopping until they hit bone. "The wound made him look like his back had been plowed," Jim said. "The other man had miraculously been able to rip his head out of a lion's mouth. But he had been partially scalped. Both men survived but only after blood transfusions and long-term wound care."

The news of the second attack produced a siege mentality in the minds of many in the district. The men would sit around their campfires at night with their spears and muzzle-loaders at the ready, facing away from the fire in the event their village was chosen for the next attack.

The women and children were protected as they sat close to the fire. The women in Marilynn's Bible study class were afraid to walk across the stream to the church because their route took them through the thick underbrush on either side of the stream, which could conceal a lion.

As the villagers sat around their campfires, surrounded by the blackness of the African night, tales of magic and the supernatural would inevitably be brought up. Sometimes those tales could be used by individuals for personal, albeit questionable, purposes.

# Danger in the Bush

For instance, Tennyson Kibungi, the hospital's X-ray man, was two hours late for work one morning. When Jim confronted him about his tardiness, he said that he had bumped into a lion on his way to work and had judiciously retreated to his home.

Jim wasn't buying that story, however. He said, "Tennyson, jump into my car, and you show me the pug marks of the lion to confirm your unlikely story."

"There won't be any tracks because it was a magic lion floating two feet above the ground," Tennyson responded with a straight face.

Jim wisely decided not to press the issue. After all, he thought, what can you say to a response like that?

The police and game guards finally managed to kill all of the man-eating lions, but not before they had attacked several other villages and completely terrorized the district. Those are the daily dangers that Africans living in the bush must face; they have no other choice. And sometimes it cost them their lives.

Missionaries in rural Africa need rest and relaxation just like everyone else. They work long hours and often face challenges unknown to most people living in the Western world. But even a day of rest in the Foulkes family's Shangri-La, a secret place on the Kabompo River 120 miles from Mukinge, proved hazardous to Jim's health—or more accurately, his life.

Jim carefully covered his tire tracks every time he drove off the main road to get to the river camping area. He wanted to make sure that no fishermen or poachers from town would discover the missionaries' secret hideout. The river was filled with large tiger fish (the fightingest game fish in Africa), and just across the large, fast-flowing river was a game reserve.

The downside of the site was that it was also an elephant crossing location because the river was shallow just at that point. Each evening at dusk, a herd would cross from the game park into the Foulkes's camp. The family would head for their vehicle, abandoning their cooking stew until the invaders had sniffed all of the motorbike seats and other human smells before heading off into the trees behind the camp. Then the displaced campers got out of their vehicle and Marilynn could finish cooking.

The herd would cross back into the park about 6:00 A.M. at a point about a quarter of a mile downstream.

There was plenty of game that lived on the same side of the river as the Foulkes camp. It was legal to hunt on that side of the river, making it possible for Jim to shoot just enough game meat to keep the stew pot full.

One morning, an elephant decided to stay on the Foulkes's side of the river until after breakfast. The jumbo was making quite a commotion while feeding on trees close to their camp. Jim decided to go and investigate.

Keeping a sharp lookout for the elephant prevented Jim from watching where he was stepping. Suddenly, his feet were thrown out from under him. He found himself bouncing up and down, with only one leg barely touching the ground at times. His other leg was up in the air.

"It took me a few seconds to realize that I was caught in a snare with a sizable cable tightly gripping my left calf. The other end of the cable was attached to a large green sapling that was strong enough to secure a one-ton Cape buffalo," Jim recalled.

Jim knew that he probably only had one chance to mobilize all of his strength to reach up and grab the cable and pull himself up.

*The boys leaving for a hunt: Milt Arnold, Gordy Bakke, Joe Faber, and Jim.*

He said, "With adrenaline pumping full blast, I thrust myself high enough to grab the cable. By pulling myself up with my arms and releasing the pressure on the slip knot of the cable, I was able to finally release my throbbing calf."

It was a close call for a man who had already exceeded his quota. He came very close to turning upside down. Had he done so, he never would have been able to right himself. Jim was also out of shouting distance from his family. His predicament seemed to parallel David's cry for help in Psalm 22:11: "Do not be far from me, for trouble is near and there is no one to help" (NIV).

But the Lord had made a way of escape from the snare. Indignant that poachers had turned his Shangri-La into a death trap for Cape buffalos—as well as humans—Jim methodically tripped every poacher's snare that he could find and threw their cables into the middle of the river. It just seemed the right thing to do. Besides that, it felt good.

# ChapterEighteen
## Battling Dark Forces

One day, while sitting in the hospital outpatient department waiting to examine the next patient, Jim suddenly felt two hands clamped around his neck in a life-threatening choke hold.

"*Bubela*! (lies)," his assailant screamed.

Jim struggled to get out of his chair, his lungs gasping for air, but his attacker shoved him back, sending both of them crashing over a table. Jim's desperate attempts to free himself and get back on his feet were futile.

The demented man thrust out a hand to gouge out an eye, but he missed his mark. Instead, his nails sliced a deep bleeding wound from a lower eyelid down the side of Jim's cheek. In the split second that the man released one hand from his throat, Jim was able to gulp in a big breath of life-saving air.

Jim was dumbfounded that he couldn't overpower this man who was a lot older and no bigger than he was. Jim's arms were well muscled from regularly playing tennis and grappling with the steering wheel of the old mission truck.

Jim vividly recalled, "I was locked into a battle for my life with a wild man, and so far I wasn't too sure but that he was succeeding. My strength was no match for that old man."

Jim was getting dizzy and felt as if he were going to black out from lack of oxygen. Then a pair of orderlies (whom he later would describe as "two of the most wonderful men in the world") rushed up and wrenched the enraged man off Jim.

Immediately, they were joined by a third orderly, but the old man threw all three men into a pile. After that, no one dared to attempt to restrain the assailant who continued yelling and cursing, adding to the pandemonium.

"Finally, Gary Byers, a big, fearless missionary, arrived with the power of the Holy Spirit shining forth from him. Gary walked right up to the wild man and the man looked into his eyes and submitted to his authority without a fight," Jim recalled.

Jim looked on the incident as a terrorizing experience with the forces of evil. He said, "I have no doubt that I had looked into eyes burning with hate and destruction, the eyes of a man displaying supernatural power while under demonic control."

The man who attacked Jim was, in fact, a former deacon in the Mukinge Church. Before his conversion, he was known as a womanizer, but for four years he had a clean record—at least as far as the church knew. In an effort to plant a church in every village, Jim had often driven him out to villages where there was no church. Jim was told by a head man of a village that the deacon had propositioned a fourteen-year-old girl in his catechumen class. After confirming that the accusation was true, Jim made sure that the straying deacon was placed under church discipline at Mukinge. "For that, he hated me," Jim said.

The disturbed man wrote several letters to Jim threatening to kill him. His threats were also directed against the Mukinge Church

*Baptismal service. No crocs in this pond, as compared to the nearby river.*

pastor. One afternoon, the pastor looked out of his window to see the man pointing a drawn bow at the pastor's son. The pastor quickly picked up his shotgun, and actually had his finger flattening the trigger to save his son's life when the crazy man let the arrow fall harmlessly from his bow.

In much of Africa, one of the great problems Westerners face is discerning true demonization or, as Jim put it, "Determining what is spurious, and what is truly out of the pit of hell."

Every day, taking histories in the hospital outpatient department, Jim asked, "How did you become sick?" Often, the answer would be that "bad spirits" had entered into the body. That probably meant that the patient just didn't understand what made him sick. And since most villagers believe nothing happens without supernatural intervention, then by default, the illness must have come from an evil spirit.

For example, among villagers, epilepsy is almost universally considered to be caused by demonic possession, as is nearly every kind of aberrant behavior. "In a land of untold multitudes of fetishes, mystery, superstition, and fear of the unknown, experience often supersedes theory," Jim explained.

Jim remembered the story of an experience that his fellow missionary and longtime friend, Steve Weiandt, had at an area church conference about a hundred miles from Mukinge.

Conferences usually occur during the cold, dry season late in August when the moon is full and the harvest has been gathered. The evenings are quite cold in August, so it is necessary to build a huge fire using timbers the size of telephone poles to keep all of the people warm. The heat from the massive campfire is so hot that no one can bear to sit closer than twenty feet from the flames. Hundreds of people sitting in many rows at a comfortable distance from the blazing fire are able to stay reasonably warm.

Steve Weiandt's eyewitness account of what happened that fateful night is well worth the telling in his own words.

My task at the annual Kabwima District Bible Conference was to relate the truths from the book of Revelation to those in attendance. I described the judgment seat of Christ, emphasizing that Christians would be judged for their earthly works to determine what rewards they would receive in heaven. Great interest was shown by all. Afterward, under the black sky, the young people performed a skit around the fire. One group role-played Christians coming before Christ and hearing what they had not done, while others took the role of the accusers. Satan and his demons were breathing accusations against the chosen, touting the things that the Christians had failed to do that God had asked them to do.

Unfortunately, the young man whose role was that of Satan seemed extremely enthusiastic about playing the part. All at once, everything seemed to break loose.

At first, we thought it was part of the performance, but then we were left trying to make sense out of what was happening. In fact, the skit had stopped and bedlam ruled. Screams erupted and fear was unloosed. Several people demonstrated signs of demon possession.

Then this seventeen-year-old boy, who was playing the part of Satan, wheeled and walked unwaveringly into the middle of that consuming, roaring fire. Even if someone had attempted a rescue, no one could have withstood the kiln-like heat. The boy just stood there, infernal, red-black flames licking about him, shaking his fist at the heavens.

He should have been burned to a cinder, but he strode out of the fire unscathed. Several men tried to restrain him, but he threw them off time and again.

People rushed up to me, asking what to do. The noise and bedlam were so great that it did not seem possible to do anything. I suggested that we bring the leadership together to pray. When we prayed, the discord and noise would go down. When we stopped praying, it increased.

Some people seemed to be delivered from demons, but not the seventeen-year-old boy. The next day when he entered the conference area, he curled up into a ball on the ground and moaned and made terrible noises.

I finally told all within earshot that he must not be allowed into the services until he was delivered. I also told them that until much prayer and fasting availed, I doubted that he would be delivered.

*The seats feel pretty hard by the end of the usual two-hour church service.*

After the conference, Steve conducted an investigation into what was going on in the Kabwima District. He found that half of the church leaders were involved in witchcraft, frequenting the witch doctors during the week and then trying to preach the gospel of light on Sunday. They were mixing the old dark ways with the new ways of Christ.

The leaders from the central church helped that sick church to come to a place of confession, repentance, and cleansing, and they were placed under church discipline. In the end, the people of the Kabwima District developed into mature Christians in their walk with the Lord.

There was no question that the seventeen-year-old boy was demonized, but often it is difficult to be sure. "A correct diagnosis in this area is critical, and yet it is often a gray area," Jim stated. When trying to diagnose a patient presenting demonic symptoms, Jim relies on criteria he believes to be set out in the New Testament.

His biblical rule of thumb to diagnose demonization is: a demonstration of supernatural strength, clairvoyance, the use of threatening language in an unknown tongue, and a strange voice coming from the demonized person that is clearly not his own.

The last criterion was demonstrated clearly by a new student nurse who, during her first week at Mukinge, became demented and whose screams upset the entire training school.

In an effort to help her, Jim and another missionary prayed for her deliverance. While reading to her from the book of 1 John about the power in the blood of Jesus Christ to cleanse, the young girl got very agitated, reached out, and tore the page out of Jim's Bible. Her controlling spirit yelled at him in a bass voice, "God I know, but who is this Jesus that you are talking about?"

Two days later this girl was gloriously saved and delivered. She lived an exemplary Christian life thereafter.

Jim confessed that he had always tried to stay as far away as possible from a deliverance ministry. "For one thing, it often required days of unremitting prayer and counsel to bring freedom to the oppressed. In my humble opinion, it is far better, by far, to spend time with the Light of the World, than to enter a shadowy, spiritual landscape and rattle sabers with the dark lord of the bottomless pit," he said.

Yet when the dark lord has one pushed into a corner at 4:00 A.M.—as were Jim and Marilynn—then the Christian must take up the sword of the Lord and do battle.

Blackson, the Foulkes's cook, came pounding on their door in a state of terror one night. While they rubbed the sleep out of their eyes, he blurted out that his wife's relatives had just arrived and wanted to forcibly whisk her off to the witch doctor to rid her of evil spirits. Blackson pleaded with Jim and Marilynn to come and exorcise his wife's evil spirits in the name and power of Jesus.

Jim recalled, "We were scared to death, yet how could we refuse, since we had been assuring Blackson and many others that God still had the same power today that He had in the days of the New Testament?"

But their heads were filled with nagging questions. They had no experience in exorcism at that time. What kind of demonstration and walk of faith would it be if they completely failed to help the demon-possessed woman? What if it didn't turn out like it did on Mount Carmel when Elijah proved to everyone that "the LORD he is God" (1 Kings 18:39)?

But even more troubling were the many stories they had heard of evil spirits coming out of the possessed and entering those who were trying to help since they were not clean vessels themselves. Weren't you supposed to fast and pray in preparing for a deliverance ministry?

They also knew there was the story of Tommy Titcomb, who was a well-intentioned, but still wet-behind-the-ears pioneer missionary in an area in Nigeria where not one tongue had professed belief in Jesus Christ.

Young Tommy walked into a witchcraft ceremony where a girl was levitating three feet off of the ground. Tommy rushed in and immediately demanded that the demons leave in the name of Christ.

As a reward for his efforts, an unseen power struck and knocked Tommy down, leaving him to lick his wounds and embarrassed that he had underestimated the enemy.

Jim and Marilynn made the decision to go, but they first wanted to meet and pray with the hospital chaplain who agreed to go with them.

"We arrived at Blackson's house with fear and trembling, our knees knocking in fellowship with each other," Jim said.

*Dr. Bill Hicks and Jim with a witch doctor who was invited into the district by the paramount chief in order to divine witches. Two old ladies that he divined as witches were later cast out of their villages and died of exposure and starvation.*

A large crowd had showed up, quickly ballooning to more than one hundred people—and still growing. Blackson's wife was on the front porch in plain sight of everyone. Her relatives seemed at the ready to carry her off if the would-be exorcists didn't make their move.

Jim, Marilynn, and the chaplain placed their hands on the troubled woman and prayed over and over for her deliverance. Many promises from the Bible were read in faith.

The clock kept ticking and nothing happened. Thirty minutes went by. The relatives grew more and more restless.

Then Marilynn believed the Holy Spirit was telling her that she should ask the troubled woman to pray. But the woman was apparently unable to even make a sound; asking her to pray seemed an exercise in futility. After many attempts, the woman finally whispered, "Dear Jesus, please help me."

The answer came. She leapt to her feet, pointing, as she said, "Don't you see them? They have all left!"

"We didn't see anything but a woman who was now clearly in her right mind," Jim said, smiling at the recollection of victory in Jesus. "She started dancing around and great praises of thanksgiving went up to Jesus and God the Father from us and many in the audience who had come to watch the show."

Marilynn and Jim were exhausted, but nevertheless thrilled that the Name had not become a laughing stock. "It is theologically clear that God's honor does not depend on our performance or faithfulness, but the theologians weren't around to teach that to our audience," Jim stated.

The spiritual struggle to deliver the woman from her evil spirits took its toll on Jim. "That experience convinced me all the more that I would dodge the ministry of deliverance whenever possible," he said.

"The Name Above All Names has the greatest power, but the dark forces have been entrenched in Africa for untold centuries, and the evil present in them should not be taken lightly," Jim advised.

Don Richardson, in his book, *Peace Child*, wrote:

You try to treat loathsome tropical diseases and run the risk of being blamed for the death of your patient if you fail . . . Most of all you must be prepared, in the strength of the Lord, to do battle with the prince of darkness, who having held these hundreds of tribes captive for many thousands of years, is not about to give them up without a fight.

How wonderful that the Father sent Jesus to be the Light of the world. Jesus said, "He that followeth Me shall not walk in darkness, but shall have the light of life" (John 8:12). For those who seek Him, the Light of the World continues to dispel the darkness.

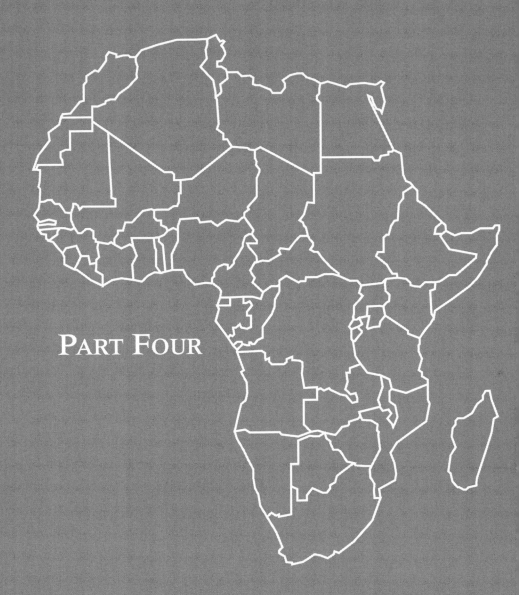

# PART FOUR

# Chapter Nineteen
## Lost!

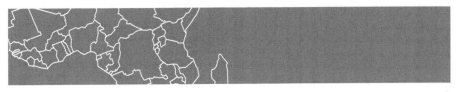

I t all began when Jim, Marilynn, and another couple, Gerry and Gloria Mudge, decided to take an Easter weekend break by riding a rubber raft down the swollen Lufupa River toward the Kafue game park.

The river normally ran through the Mukinge mission property as a calm, narrow stream; but exceptionally heavy rains had turned the waterway into a roaring torrent of brown froth that widened to a half mile in places. In 1969, the wet season of December through March nearly doubled its regular rainfall output of forty-three inches.

April came, and instead of the rains gradually petering out, the daily downpours became even more heavy. The single dirt road leading to Mukinge from town had been shut down for two months, blocked by a fleet of trucks hopelessly mired in the deep, glue-like mud.

All of the schools and hospitals in the province which relied on that one road for supplies had run out of fuel and food and could no longer pump water or feed students and patients. A single-engine plane airlift by bush pilot Gordon Bakke brought in the vital supplies which kept Mukinge Hospital and the station's secondary school in operation.

But the bad news kept piling up. Several local school children drowned while attempting to cross swollen streams. One young lad, fishing on the main road in two feet of water, was taken by a crocodile.

Looking at the raging river, Jim was reminded of the days of his youth in Lima, Ohio, when the spring floods beckoned him to get out his canoe and challenge the white water. Jim was very much at home in a canoe. As a twenty-year-old Eagle Scout, he had been the waterfront director at the district scout camp.

# To Africa with Love

The evening before embarking on their adventure, Jim and Gerry drove Jim's pickup truck to a spot fifteen miles from Mukinge. They parked the truck on a little side road leading to the edge of the river and left it where it could be easily seen from the river. They then returned to base on a motorbike.

The plan called for the four to leisurely raft down the river to where the truck was, then to drive back to Mukinge before dark.

At 8:00 A.M. on Saturday, the four adventurers put their rubber raft into the rapidly racing river. The conditions looked ideal for an exciting time, and the sun was shining for the first time in many days, which seemed to be a good omen.

The fast current whipped the raft along at breakneck speed, filling the passengers with joy and excitement. Even with all of the river's twists and turns, they had hoped to arrive at the site of the pickup truck by early afternoon. By three o'clock, however, it became obvious that they were still a long way from their vehicle.

Jim recalled, "At that point, we made the only smart decision of the adventure—we sent our wives to walk back on a major path that intersected the course of the river. Gerry and I carried on in good spirits, fully confident that we would reach our truck by sunset."

Marilynn and Gloria had not wanted to leave because they were enjoying, à la Huck Finn, the pleasant afternoon on the raft. But they were persuaded that it would be better for them to get back to Mukinge to look after the children and to tell others that Jim and Gerry were safe and would soon be back home.

Soon after their wives departed, the twosome found their carefree enjoyment giving way to careworn anxiety as they started running into bigger problems than they had ever imagined.

The wild water had risen to treetop height, fifteen or twenty feet above normal levels. As a consequence, a gauntlet of tree limbs stretched out several feet above the river's surface, waiting to wallop in the head anyone who would draw near. Jim and Gerry were repeatedly bounced out of the rubber raft into the muddy torrent whenever the hapless raft crashed into a low-lying tree limb.

Fortunately, each time that happened, one or the other was able to cling to the inside of the raft. Then began the struggle to drag the poor man overboard out of the raw power of the flood waters before he was swept away by the torrent.

# Lost!

Another troublesome problem emerged—the tree branches had become the final refuge of a large number of snakes trapped by the water. Unable to control the raft's direction in the turbulent waters, both Jim and Gerry sent silent prayers upward every time their rubber raft sailed perilously close to a branch bearing a serpent.

An even bigger problem lay ahead. The picturesque, flat-topped acacia trees that grace the plains of Zambia brandish long sharp thorns. Dashed against the upper limbs of these thorny trees several times, one side of the raft ripped open, instantly deflating the compartment.

Jim quickly grabbed the repair kit that they had thoughtfully brought along for emergencies. Upon opening the kit, they discovered that it was designed to repair only pin holes, not major rips. With three-fourths of the raft still inflated, they managed to stay afloat for another hour before another thorny tree skewered the raft, causing a second section to blow.

The two men were forced to straddle the four-foot-long section of the raft that remained inflated, which had the diameter of a telephone pole. This required the men to dangle their feet in the current.

"The only thing rushing faster than the water at this point was the pace of our hearts, knowing that we were very tempting croc food in a river teeming with the critters," Jim remembered.

By sunset, the two soaking wet and weary missionaries had to make a decision: Abandon the raft and strike out cross country for the road that they figured must be about ten miles straight west or set up camp at riverside for the night and carry on downriver the next morning, hoping to reach their vehicle.

Both men were desperate for warmth and rest. They put ashore. As any veteran camper knows, one of the most important factors in survival when lost in the woods is the ability to make a fire. They had matches and were finally able to spark a fire with wet wood. But within an hour, a drenching rain came down, extinguishing the feeble flames. Soaked to the bone, they knew they couldn't just sit there shivering all night without a fire, waiting for the inevitable hypothermia to set in. So they started walking in pitch darkness without a compass toward what they hoped would be the road.

They were grateful to God for delivering them from the dangerous animals that owned the river—snakes, crocs, and hippos.

While they made their way through the thick, sharp-edged elephant grass, they prayed for further protection from hungry, flesh-eating lions and leopards.

Somehow, they managed to tramp all night, eagerly awaiting the first rays of sunlight, which would answer the nagging question—were they indeed walking westward?

By 6:00 A.M., the sky was still pelting down big drops of cold rain. A solid gray blanket of clouds hung low like a huge veil blotting out the sun, so they were unable to tell within 180 degrees from where the source of light came.

A few hours later, they stumbled into a huge barrier, hearing the rush of it before seeing it through a tangled green mat of dense bush. It was the roaring of the Lufupa River itself. After walking all night in the darkness, they were now back at the very same river from whence they had begun.

At this point, they had to admit the obvious: they were hopelessly lost—and worn out. Their spirits were as deflated as the ripped raft they had hung on a tree limb. The possibility remained, however, that the river had taken a wide loop and that they were still more or less on course. If this were true, they would have to swim across the river to get to the road.

They dove into the river, keeping an eye out for the swirl of water that could mean a hungry croc or an angry hippo. Swimming as hard as they could, they found that the fast-moving, swollen river quickly sapped their strength. They had badly underestimated the time and effort it would take to cross the wild Lufupa. The short swim in the river had also waterlogged their matches, and Jim feared it had also ruined the bullets in his pistol.

About noon, a sound spread through the sodden sky that was literally music to their ears—the drone of the mission Cessna plane that had been sent out to search for the pair.

Their hopes were dashed when they realized that pilot Gordon Bakke could never see them while they were under the canopy of trees. They felt even more helpless because they couldn't build a fire, and they had no kind of mirror to reflect the light as a signal to the pilot.

From up above, Gordy did spot their truck, making it obvious that they were somewhere between Mukinge and the truck. But, dead or alive?

And while it was only fifteen air miles from the truck to the station, for them it was more than thirty miles of raging river and wild, uninhabited bush country.

The two wanderers could only stand and watch as the plane droned off into the distance. Dispirited, but still believing, they prayed God would guide them to the road.

Deep concern for the missing men mounted every hour back at Mukinge Station. Physical therapist Joy Warner kept a diary of those desperate days:

> *Last night, I climbed into bed at 3:00 A.M., after Ness and I had returned from seeing the three men who had set out on motor-bikes across the semi-flooded bridge at Kasempa, to go in search for Jim and Gerry.*
>
> *This morning, as I looked out at the Kikonkomene hill from my bedroom window, it looked to me grotesque and forbidding. Somewhere, the Bush Queen of Africa was hiding our loved ones, helpless in her beautiful but cruel grasp.*
>
> *The heavy mist lifted a little, and the top of the hill could be seen in the pink sunrise. To me, this was as if the Lord was lifting a corner of the veil of silent mystery, and somehow our men would come back today.*

Jim knew that it was time to reevaluate their situation. Both were near exhaustion from exposure, lack of sleep, and the long jungle trek through the thick elephant grass. They had so many angry blisters on their feet, that every step was filled with pain.

But their greatest concern was their wives. They knew they would be sick with worry. Both men had done a lot of praying, and each prayer included a plea that the Lord would somehow let their loved ones know that they were still alive.

Jim remembered, "Our little adventure had turned into a disaster, and instead of taming the wilds, the wilds had tamed us. In a matter of hours, the beauty of the jungle wilderness surrounding us had been transformed into an object of dread."

Dread came in many forms. Late in the day, they heard the loud noise of a great beast storming through the bush, headed in their direction. An elephant came crashing through the high grass and rushed right by them. A close call.

Once again, God had protected them from deadly harm. A good thing, too, since the men would not have been able to run very far or fast—even from an angry elephant—because of their tender feet and marked weakness.

Jim pulled off one of his water-soaked, ill-fitting tennis shoes and threw it away, considering that he would do better without the shoe that had rubbed so many blisters on his foot. Gerry fared no better. He had cut open the toes of his shoes in an attempt to make walking less painful.

The elephant grass was one of their biggest enemies. The long, rainy season had made the stalks as thick as a human thumb and higher than an elephant's eye. Jim and Gerry could lean their full weight against the wall of the dense grass without bending it over. Gerry's legs were slashed to ribbons by the tall, sharp grass; he had elected to wear shorts rather than long trousers for what was supposed to be an afternoon floating lazily downstream.

The men had devoured their last sandwich the day before. Their stomachs growled constantly while their limbs grew weak from the strain, the cold, and the lack of food. Water was no problem since there were puddles everywhere.

As the more experienced of the two in braving the bush— "Jungle Jim" had been in Zambia for ten years, Gerry less than one—Jim began to blame himself for their problems. He had always been able to cope with any challenge that he had faced in the jungle since he always took a bush-savvy local hunter with him.

This time it was just two *bazungu* (white men), and neither one of them could survive alone. A serious break in their bond of trust, one with the other, would doom them both.

"Gerry had great courage and never once expressed any anger toward me, but I had gotten us into this mess, and I was unable to extricate us from our jungle prison," Jim said later, with great gratitude for Gerry.

Their only option was to push on. To survive, they had to keep their core temperature up to stave off the violent shaking and hypothermia that would come in the cold grasp of the wet night.

At sunset on Sunday—the end of the second day—they got a good bearing on the West, but it didn't do them any good. They were forced to stumble along through the black night, not really knowing where they were.

The nights were the hardest. The darkness is almost palpable in Africa. They knew that every time they took a step they could be placing a foot on a snake.

Early Monday morning, forty-eight hours after setting out from home, they again heard the plane searching for them. When the plane finished its criss-crossing and turned back toward Mukinge, their hearts sank to their lowest point. They could only think of their wives anxiously waiting at the airstrip, only to be told more bad news.

They felt totally hopeless and impotent, but somehow they managed to muster enough strength to keep walking.

Joy wrote:

> *Gordon took off in the plane at 6:00 A.M. to search from the air again and look for another prearranged signal made by the men who had gone out from Mukinge on motorbikes . . . Marilynn went too.*

> *Heard Gordon come in about 7:00 A.M., so everyone headed for the air strip—No, there was no sign of them. Len, Dick, and Milton had arrived at Jim's car, but there was no trace of Gerry and Jim. Marilynn looked dreadful. The sight of the density of the bush, swamps, and rivers everywhere hit her afresh. But an hour later she was at the hospital, carrying on as usual.*

Marilynn may have been carrying on as usual at the hospital, but when the plane had returned, she broke down and sobbed in the privacy of their home. Their little four-year-old Jackie ran up to her mother and asked: "Why are you crying, Mommy?"

Marilynn put her arms around her, "Daddy's lost in the bush."

"Don't worry, Mommy. Jesus will find him just like He found the little lost sheep." Jackie put down her little security blanket that normally stayed welded to her hands, and ran to get her Bible story book to prove that Jesus did, indeed, find lost sheep.

The rest of the morning, the two men slowly trudged through the jungle, barely able to put one foot in front of the other. By early afternoon, they knew that they couldn't possibly walk through another night or day. Physically exhausted and emotionally drained, they feared that if it rained any more that night, they would be unable to stave off the effects of exposure to the wet and chill.

If they could only make it through the night, and get some rest the next morning, they might survive by eating raw frog's legs or other similar delicacies available in the bush.

For the first time, they faced squarely the strong possibility that they were going to die. They inhaled the cold dewy air into their lungs and exhaled prayers, beseeching God to hold off the rain and save their lives.

Joy wrote:

> *All throughout that day a hushed atmosphere prevailed at the hospital. The men stood around in groups, and nurses, too.*
>
> *Our hearts were heavy indeed. Everyone knew the secret fears which lurked in every mind. The Africans spoke quite openly about the dangers of anyone—especially Europeans—getting*

*lost in an uninhabitable area such as the one where the men must be.*

*Still, the spirits kept up, with Gloria and Marilynn showing unparalleled courage and faith. Ginger came down to the hospital and said that the district secretary was organizing the police and men at the boma into search parties, and others would do the same from here.*

As the darkness crept toward them, Jim and Gerry believed this, their third night, could very well be their last. But then, quite suddenly, they stumbled upon one of the most beautiful sights they had ever seen—the fresh footprints of a small child! They knew that following those small footprints would lead them to a fishing encampment—and thence to safety. Isaiah 11:6 flashed into Jim's mind: "and a little child shall lead them."

With adrenaline they never knew they had left, they were pumped up enough to push their beaten bodies onward, their eyes straining in the semidarkness to follow those little footprints.

"Within twenty minutes we came up on the glow of a fire, and sitting around the life-giving warmth were four of the most lovely-looking people I could ever have imagined," Jim recalled years later, still with excitement in his voice.

The four Kaonde fishermen had heard that the two missionaries were lost via the bush telegraph. Fortunately, Jim could talk to the men in their own language.

"They seemed to be as happy to see us as we were to see them, but it would have been impossible to outshine the joy that we were experiencing at that moment. Our loving and ever-present Father received a lot of praise that night (and for many days to come) for sustaining us," Jim said.

The fishermen prepared a feast of thick porridge and fish for their starving and exhausted guests. Jim would later call it a "miracle meal." Afterwards, filled with food and somewhat rested, Jim and Gerry told their hosts they were anxious to get word back to Mukinge that they were still alive and safe.

"Would any of the men consider serving as their guide?" No one would. It was too dangerous in lion country and with swollen streams.

The two missionaries were disappointed, but nothing could mar the happiness and relief of knowing that, on the morrow, they would be back home with their loved ones.

Sleeping on the ground by a blazing fire, driving the cold out of their bones and drying their wet clothes, caused Jim and Gerry to feel like they were lying in the lap of luxury. No king-sized mattress in a five-star hotel could have felt better.

At first light on Tuesday, they scribbled notes to their wives and sent them off with a fisherman on his bicycle. They, sore of foot with muscles aching, started their slow, tortuous trek across the eight miles separating them from the road. This time, their newfound guides made sure they didn't get lost again.

Seeing how painful it was for the two men to walk on their ulcerated feet, the Africans took pity, put them on their two remaining bicycles, and pushed them along the path leading to the road.

Joy wrote:

*We gathered as usual for 10:00 A.M. prayers. The reading for the day was Psalm 37:4: "Delight yourself in the Lord and He will give you the desires of your heart" (NIV).*

*As Doraine closed the study, a motorbike roared up to the hospital, and we could hear Gordy's excited voice. He had met a fisherman with a note from Jim saying that they were walking toward the Njenga.*

*Pent up feelings burst forth. Africans poured into the front of the hospital from all quarters. The nurses were screaming for joy. The word flew!*

*Gordon and I hastily wrote out a bunch of notes to be dropped from the plane, telling the three missionaries who had gone out the night before of Jim's request to bring back the truck. It didn't take Gordon long to get off of the ground with Nachi and one of the policemen.*

*Meanwhile, we returned to the office for coffee and a time of thanksgiving. There wasn't a dry eye among us. This was more than overwhelming joy at the news of the fellows safety; it was deep humble gratitude to God for His abundant answer to the ceaseless prayers of His people both black and white. Anguish of heart had drawn the cords of love tightly, as nothing else can.*

*When the plane returned shortly, they were overjoyed at actually having seen the two men on the bicycles and their African escort. Ginger and Uncle Ernie jumped in the car and headed out to meet the party.*

*12:30 P.M.—Screams coming from the direction of the Foulkes house, along with a total depopulation of the hospital and surrounding district, led us all on the double over to the house. What a sight! Oh, what love!*

Jim and Gerry stood at the back-door steps, Jim supported by Marilynn, and Gerry swaying a little uncertainly. Almost unrecognizable, their eyes glazed, their clothes filthy, Jim with one shoe missing and a dirty rag tied around his ankle; Gerry in shorts, his legs lashed and bleeding from the cutting grass. But they were both smiling.

The mob of Africans and missionaries surged forward to grasp their hands or hug them. Rather than being treated like the way they looked—a couple of old rag pickers—they were lifted like royalty and carried on the shoulders of the people of Mukinge for "far too long a time" (according to Jim). The teeming crowd danced and shouted praises to God. What a wonderful resurrection!

Joy continued:

*The African bush had been compelled to relinquish her treasure because the prayers of the faithful prevailed, and united confidence in our loving Father was rewarded.*

# To Africa with Love

Jim said:

When all the hugs had been passed around, we found out that we were not the only ones who uttered *"twa lala ne, twa ja ne"* (we have not slept, we have not eaten). Many friends—black and white—had not slept or eaten—fasting and praying through the nights that we were missing—until God answered their prayers.

We had come to the people of Africa to minister to their needs in the name of the Lord Jesus, and now we were the ones receiving the blessing.

The Good Shepherd had found His two lost sheep; now they were safely back in the fold. Hurting hearts had been healed; loved ones reunited.

To God be the glory!

# Chapter**Twenty**
## Faith at Home and Abroad

I t was 1970, a wonderful year for the Foulkes. They were going back to Ohio for the first time in five years. Marilynn rejoiced in a letter dated Christmas of 1970:

*I just love being a housewife in America. What fun it is to be able to buy anything a recipe calls for, to have twenty-four-hour electricity, unlimited water, ready-made clothes for the children: these are some of the bonuses we're enjoying.*

*But Africa is still deep in our hearts.*

The family left Mukinge in May, and the trip home was long and tedious by design. The time was spent camping around Europe in a VW camper with a tent. They visited the ancient salt mine in Austria, a flower auction in Holland, a night stop atop the Jungfrau in the Swiss Alps, and the passion play at Oberammagau, Germany.

Jim's mother had rented an old farmhouse, "all cleaned and cozied up," for them to move into when they arrived in Lima. The house was surrounded by woods and fields.

Marilynn was elated that the children could go to school on a bus, "sparing them the trauma of being thrust into an unknown world of traffic and stoplights. And their Mommy will never forget this present joy of kissing them good-bye in the morning, knowing that they'll be home later that afternoon, and not four months later."

While in Lima, Jim spent his time speaking in churches and working on correspondence and mission business. But like an old fire horse, he couldn't stay out of the saddle long. He started working in the emergency room of a local hospital so that he could "keep [his] hand in."

# To Africa with Love

Marilynn was involved in a weekly Bible study/coffee hour, studying the book of Romans. It was a great opportunity to solidify the faith of women, a number of whom were married to Jim's special friends in Lima.

Jim was also able to contact some recruits for African service. Gwennie took guitar lessons for the first time. Jill and Jackie were taught music by an old Foulkes family friend, Marge Hollinger. Terrie and Gwennie had the delight of visiting an American dentist.

But furloughs go fast, so in May of 1971, Marilynn wrote:

*We're just off on our way back to Zambia. We fly from Dayton to Costa Rica, where we'll spend a week getting reacquainted with the Dick Foulkes family. Then we hope to work our way south and east across South America to Rio, where there is a flight across to Africa. One of the fringe benefits of being a missionary is the necessity of becoming a world traveler.*

*You might be interested in some American luxuries we'll shortly be pining for: cottage cheese, fresh milk, public libraries, lights on all night, long-distance phone service, hamburger joints, English-language services with organ music, and the light green smell of spring.*

*But soon, we'll have the exciting privilege of joining again the vital young Zambian church in the work of evangelism. With the prospect of new staff at the hospital, Jim hopes to be able to move around the district more with the thrust of preventive medicine and evangelism. This has long been Jim's dream.*

The Foulkeses had a more difficult time in getting back to Zambia than they had in leaving it. The trouble started after the flight from Brazil to South Africa. In Johannesburg airport, they learned that they were not confirmed for the fifteen-hundred-mile trip north to Zambia. Every flight was already booked because of the school holidays.

They spent several long, frustrating days, going to the airport each day, hoping to get six standby seats to Zambia, and eventually realized that it was an impossibility. The next best thing was to rent a car and drive as far as Victoria Falls, on the border of Rhodesia and Zambia, entering the country by land. Because

*Dr. Bob and Carol Wenninger, beloved colleagues who shared the burdens and joys of Mukinge Hospital with the Foulkes family for twenty-seven years.*

of the hostilities between those two countries, however, they had to leave their rented car on the Rhodesian side of the falls, unload their nineteen bags, and trudge with the luggage just over a mile through no-man's-land to the customs office on the Zambian side. That took a total of three hours with required multiple trips.

They then had to face an all-night train journey to Lusaka, the Zambian capital. It so happened that the train was loaded with drunks and several of those under the influence gave the weary travelers a hard time. The crowning blow, however, came abruptly at 4:00 A.M., when a load of iron cooking pots came crashing down on Jim's head, knocking him semiconscious. There were some choice words exchanged.

The final lap of their long journey was the 450-mile drive from Lusaka to Mukinge. The family was tired and completely worn out from the long ride, but thrilled when the car turned onto the familiar road. Mukinge at last!

As they drove up to their house, the surrounding hospital grounds were covered with remembered faces, waiting to see, sing, and embrace. People came with eggs, vegetables, and chickens as love gifts. Their beloved physician and family were home.

*Marilynn's language class, introducing new missionaries pilot Gordon Bakke and Dr. Camille Jamison to the strange sounds of Kikaonde.*

When Jim got back in the swing of things at the hospital, he was delighted to see some new faces. God had sent much-needed reinforcements while they were gone. Dr. Bob Wenninger had arrived to take up the slack caused by Jim's absence at the hospital, and to reinforce Dr. Camille Jamison.

Bob had a gift and love for surgery as did Camille, so that allowed Jim to relinquish the time-consuming duties of elective surgery. There was still the administrative work to be done, however. Some of the Zambian staff were upset that the hospital could not match the salary increases awarded by government hospitals.

Marilynn described her husband's frustration with the increasing burden of administration duties at the hospital in another letter home: "Jim continues to be a reluctant draftee on too many committees, and he would rather be a do-er than a talker."

Marilynn's teaching load included lesson preparation for Sunday school teachers, Bible study groups with African women, language lessons for new missionaries, and choir practice for the student nurses. They were starting a new term with their plates full, maybe even running over!

But Marilynn wrote:

*I am enthusiastic about all the possibilities at this point. I hope they won't ever become just a bunch of duties. That verse in Ephesians about "redeeming the time" has been in my mind constantly. We've got so many wonderful opportunities in Zambia right now, it would be awful to waste them.*

And waste them, they didn't.

The following year saw them involved in a nationwide evangelistic crusade that was to feature three Ugandans as keynote speakers. Unfortunately, these eagerly awaited, godly churchmen were not able to obtain the necessary exit visas from their troubled country, then under the harsh rule of dictator Idi Amin, who had just murdered the keynote speaker's bishop.

The crusade went ahead anyway, and God was able to work through the local Christian leaders who stood up instead. During the evangelistic crusade at Kasempa, the local boma, three hundred people publicly acknowledged Christ as their Savior. The excitement peaked on the climactic last night when an important local political leader, for whom many had prayed, had it announced over the loudspeakers that: "Dickson Bweupe wants everyone to know that he has come back to the Lord!"

In preparation for the crusade, Marilynn, along with others, trained about eighty counselors to speak individually with those moved to make a decision for Christ. While working with the women's classes, she witnessed some amazing transformations, as the women became bolder in speaking out for the Lord.

But revival rarely comes without a fight. Around that time, tribalism, often simmering under the surface, was beginning to cause strife amongst the student nurses.

Marilynn related how she went to a class one morning and found every girl in tears! They were so upset that teaching them was impossible. She dismissed the class and, after praying about it, arranged to meet with them the same evening.

At the meeting, she spoke about the two sides of forgiveness, God forgiving them for their wrongs against Him, and their forgiving others for wrongs done to them. The students were quiet as the message slowly sank in.

Marilynn related: "After they were dismissed, the students started coming back in tears, asking us to pray and to help them get their lives straightened out. That night, instead of insults and party spirit, hymns of praise and joy could be heard around the hospital compound."

Meanwhile, the Foulkes girls were entering their teenage years. They continued to be away at boarding school for long periods. With Terrie, the eldest, leading the way, one-by-one they graduated from grade school at Sakeji to high school at Rift Valley Academy (RVA), a boarding school located on the escarpment near Nairobi, Kenya, fifteen hundred miles to the north of Mukinge.

With a brand new four-by-four vehicle, bouncing over the miles to church meetings in the surrounding area became much easier. It was not long before the family decided to try out their new "wheels" on a long distance safari. So, in 1972, they drove overland through the country of Tanzania to pick up Terrie at the end of her school year at RVA.

*Getting ready to leave after a village church conference. That's Auntie Marge in the straw hat.*

They went in convoy with a group of missionaries from Mukinge. As always, camping along the way added a touch of the unpredictable, which served to unite them further as a family, as they shared in experiencing Mother Nature's wildness alongside of man's mischief.

The thrills of game-viewing and the natural beauty of the land were offset by the menace of marauding bandits, always on the lookout for unsuspecting tourists to prey upon. In those days as now, a brand new four-by-four vehicle would fetch thousands of dollars on the black market, no questions asked!

Nevertheless, along with Aunties Joy and Marge, and the Ayletts, they enjoyed many of the famous sights in East Africa. Experiencing the likes of the Serengeti Plain proved to be a welcome compensation for the pressures of life on the mission compound.

# Chapter Twenty-one
## Healthcare, African-style

Stories of persons bitten by killer snakes are rarely highlighted in missionary letters for fear of hurting staff recruiting and scaring away visitors. The truth is, that of the twenty to twenty-five snakebite victims admitted annually to Mukinge Hospital, all but a handful are discharged within seventy-two hours with just local swelling and pain.

Jim recalled an incident involving a friend who struggled about going to Africa with her surgeon husband because of her fear of snakes. Then one day she almost stepped on a rattlesnake on her own front porch in Arizona. Realizing that danger could lurk at home as well as in Africa helped her decide to go. The couple spent much of their retirement serving the Lord at mission hospitals in Africa.

On the flip side, years later, Jim remarked, "It was a bit humorous for us to hear that our young African-born and bred grandchildren were nervous about coming to the United States on furlough. 'Don't they have bears in America?' they would say in hushed tones."

Jim was often called to the student nurses' quarters or to individual homes when they discovered a snake. The spitting cobra was the most common invader of human turf; the hollow fangs of the cobra allow it to shoot its highly irritating venom right into the eyes of its enemies with amazing pin-point accuracy. Jim always wore goggles when he hunted for cobras; he had treated too many villagers with red, inflamed eyes after being hit with venom. "Fortunately, this type of cobra prefers to spit rather than bite," Jim noted.

In Africa, chickens usually sound the first nocturnal alert that something is wrong. The four most likely reasons chickens become agitated and make a ruckus are: a thief, a wildcat, an attack of tens of thousands of army ants, or a spitting cobra. If it was the last one,

Jim would sometimes get an urgent call for help. "Doctor, please come and bring your gun!"

Several times when Jim first entered a darkened chicken house in answer to an SOS call, his first clue of the snake's position was when a flood of poison splashed off of his goggles and drained down onto his cheek. Thanks to the snake's warning, Jim could then take charge.

Once Jim responded to a call for help from the girls' secondary school. He found the entire student body of five hundred boarders throwing rocks at an enormous cobra.

The tail of the cobra was still on the road, but it was moving fast toward the side of it. The head was ready to dive into a big hole in the side of a giant, ten-foot-high anthill, and it was obvious that the snake would soon be safe in its catacombs.

Because Jim could plainly see the head of the snake, he thought it safe to grab the tail and hold the creature down in order to kill it. Jim looked around for a rock. He had come on the scene hurriedly, and had neither goggles nor his gun, but there was quite a collection of rocks that the schoolgirls had hurled at the snake.

Grabbing the snake's tail, however, failed to stop its progress. Befuddled, Jim gave a great jerk on the tail in his hand. At that moment, the snake split apart into two pieces.

Initially confused about what was happening, Jim realized he was holding the tail of a snake whose head was only a step away from his feet! At that point, five hundred schoolgirls went screaming toward their dorms.

Jim dropped the tail, and used the largest rock he could find to crush the snake's head. When the rest of the long cobra slithered into the safety of the anthill, it became clear what had happened. Apparently, they had disturbed a hungry, aggressive seven-foot cobra in the process of swallowing a six-foot cobra.

Jim recalled, with a chuckle, "In retrospect, the distance from the tail on the road to the head on the anthill was much too long for a cobra, but in the land of magic snakes, anything can happen."

One of the first patients Jim saw at Mukinge was Paul Reid, the resident game ranger for the Kasempa District, who had been bitten by a black mamba. A herpetologist at heart, the ranger spent some

*This uninvited guest is a six-foot spitting cobra that invaded the Foulkes's home along with its mate. The mate was killed immediately, but this one hid in a spare bedroom for three days before appearing in the sitting room. When it was discovered, the cobra raised up two feet and hooded before being killed.*

of his time in the bush collecting venomous snakes. He could sell the live snakes to European zoos for a price that reportedly exceeded his salary from the game department. As a result, he generously rewarded the game guards under his command when they caught a venomous snake and delivered it to him in good condition.

But even professional snake handlers can get bitten. While transferring a twelve-foot mamba from a gunny sack to a cage, the aggressive snake bit Paul's finger through the sack.

The ranger knew that if he did not get help quickly he could die. He immediately grabbed two fellow officers who drove him the three miles from the government center to Mukinge Hospital. On the way, Paul yanked out his penknife and started to saw away at the bitten finger. The accompanying officer assumed that Paul had gone berserk, so he wrestled the knife from his hand and threw it out the window.

Actually, Paul's action was perfectly rational. He knew that amputating the finger within a few minutes of the bite might eliminate enough venom to save his life. The terrible pain from the venom had already spread to his armpit. He knew that within another minute or two, his chest would become involved.

Once the poison paralyzes the intercostal muscles, breathing becomes impossible. The muscles that allow swallowing are also paralyzed. The profuse outpouring of saliva, combined with the inability to swallow, brings on death by choking and drowning in one's own secretions.

The Land Rover bearing the ranger came roaring to the front of the hospital with horn blaring. Fortunately, Dr. Bob Foster was there, and immediately took charge of the situation. By that time, Paul was no longer able to breathe. Only nine or ten minutes had passed since the bite had taken place. If the hospital had been another mile away, the ranger would have been dead on arrival.

Dr. Foster quickly got Paul into the operating room, cleared his airway, and started assisted breathing. Many anxious hours crawled by before the ranger could breathe on his own. The finger that Paul had tried unsuccessfully to amputate became gangrenous five days later. The veteran Dr. Foster turned to his newly arrived assistant and asked Jim to finish the job of amputating the dead finger under anesthesia.

Paul and his wife, Joan, were greatly shaken by his near-death encounter. They had a real conviction that God had spared his life for some reason, and they were deeply grateful.

"They returned their thanks to Him in the best way possible, by committing their lives to Christ. Paul passed from death to life in more ways than one that day," Jim said.

Encounters with mambas, though rare, are greatly feared—and rightly so. Jim often tells the story of fellow missionary Roy Comrie, who was bitten by a black mamba and became one of the few who lived to tell the tale.

Roy had been walking around the airstrip to make sure that the grass had been cut properly. On the way back to his house, Roy suddenly slumped to the ground in agony. The pain shooting up his leg was so intense that, at first, he thought that he must have been shot by a bullet.

The unseen attacker, now five yards away, raised its ugly head three feet above the ground and started swaying back and forth, all the while looking intently at his prey.

Roy knew snakes well. The snake looking at him was the fastest moving, quickest-killing snake in Africa. It can rise high enough off of the ground to bite a man in the face. When Roy saw the twelve-foot mamba, his first thought was, *I'm dead!*

The mamba slithered toward him for a second bite since its victim was not dying fast enough. Roy knew that getting up and hobbling toward home would cause the venom to circulate more rapidly and would hasten his death. But just sitting there, waiting to be bitten again, was not an acceptable option.

Hopping along, he felt the pain and weakness begin its deadly climb up his leg. The snake left him alone as he kept hopping, all the while praying that he might reach home before the neurotoxin paralyzed his respiratory muscles. By the time he reached his house, he was barely conscious.

Roy's wife, Gwynneth, controlling her terror long enough to perform the only medical intervention that she knew to do, injected half an ampoule of universal antivenin into the area around the bite. Then with her hands shaking almost uncontrollably, she managed to inject the other half intramuscularly.

Unfortunately, in those early days, effective antivenin specifically against the venom of the black mamba was unavailable. Gwynneth's valiant effort had been in vain. There was no hospital nearby. Even if Roy could have been moved, his chances for recovery were nil. But as many believers can testify, "man's extremity becomes God's opportunity," and, indeed, at this point, only a miracle could save Roy's life.

When word of the mamba bite reached the Bible school, the students rushed over to the Comries's house and started a prayer meeting. The students cried out to God to save the life of their beloved principal. Whenever Roy lapsed into unconsciousness, the prayer volume increased and the fervency of the prayers would reach heaven, and Roy would come around again.

"These godly young men prayed Roy through the night, and they reversed that fatal bite by holding onto God, hour after hour," Jim said.

Miraculously, by morning, Roy was able to breathe well. It was a time of great rejoicing that the Father had answered their pleas for a celestial antivenin necessary to save his life.

Jim's expertise with treating snakebites was tested much later in his career when a peaceful afternoon was interrupted by an SOS call suddenly blared over the radio intercom. Mark Frew had been visciously bitten by a snake and was lapsing in and out of consciousness.

Mark, the twenty-six-year-old son of veteran missionaries Keith and Cindy Frew, had returned to the mission station at Chizera, revisiting the land of his youth with his bride and young son.

While walking in an open field, an unseen snake, feared to be a black mamba, had lashed out and sunk its fangs deeply into Mark's heel, leaving him envenomated with a lethal amount of poison.

The mission at Chizera had an airstrip, but it was a hundred miles from Mukinge. After receiving the SOS, Jim rushed to the hospital refrigerator where the vaccines and antisera were stored. Much to his horror, he could not find any pooled tropical snake antivenin (by this time the pooled antivenin had some antivenom effective against the black mamba). He quickly grabbed some first aid materials and rushed to the plane, with only thirty minutes of fading light left in the day to make the thirty-minute flight to Chizera.

As Don Amborski, the mission pilot and Jim's son-in-law, skillfully brought the plane onto the air strip, Jim prayed that he wouldn't find Mark with symptoms of neurotoxicity from the bite of a mamba. The lethal venom from such a bite would leave the victim strangling in his own secretions, forcing them to immediately load Mark—if he were still alive—into the plane and risk a dangerous night landing back at Mukinge.

Keeping someone alive who has been bitten by a mamba often requires a tracheotomy and long-term respiratory assistance for the scant few who ever reach the hospital in time. Jim is not a pessimist, but he could remember only five cases in which he was sure the victims had been bitten by a black mamba and who had actually reached the hospital alive. The black mamba is called, with only a little exaggeration, the twelve-step snake, because that is often as far as the bitten victim can go before dropping dead.

After the plane had landed at Chizera, a worried crowd of over one hundred people parted to reveal Mark lying on the ground outside the Frew home, where the pain had just overwhelmed him. He was conscious, but in severe pain and his foot was rapidly swelling.

Jim could see by looking at Mark that he was suffering no excessive secretions, no shallow breathing, no drooping of the eyelids, nor twitching muscles. He breathed a sigh of relief. He knew that Mark had been bitten by a viper rather than by a neurotoxic snake.

Jim still had a life-threatening problem to deal with. He only had enough medical supplies to keep Mark out of shock, but narcotics were desperately needed to ease his excruciating pain. Another SOS call went over the radio to Mukinge for narcotics, and they were delivered by Land Rover later that night.

By morning, the swelling of Mark's ankle and calf was so severe that Jim worried that he might have to make relaxing incisions to relieve the pressure in the inner compartments of Mark's leg in order to maintain the blood supply. Jim was fairly certain, based on Mark's symptoms, that he had been bitten by a Gabon viper. The bite pierced through his running shoe, the fangs not stopping until they hit bone. A Gabon viper, with its two-and-a-half-inch-long fangs, can produce as much as a cup of venom, capable of killing a grown man within fifteen minutes with one bite.

Early the next morning they loaded Mark onto the plane and flew him to Mukinge. But by day four, his condition had worsened. Mark was confused and was oozing blood from the fang holes and the IV insertion sites. His blood was failing to clot due to the hemolytic actions of the venom, and he began requiring multiple transfusions of whole blood.

Mark was also hemorrhaging into his kidneys. Concerned that he would hemorrhage into other vital organs, the decision was made to air-vac him to Johannesburg (Joburg). Jim feared that Mark might require a below-the-knee amputation.

In the intensive-care unit in Joburg, a surgical team pumped in antibiotics, excised dead skin and muscle, and carefully monitored his kidney function. After many days of intensive care and the unremitting prayer of many, Mark finally began to improve. Though he required ankle-to-thigh skin grafting and intensive physical therapy, Mark gradually improved to the point where he could be discharged.

When Mark returned to Chizera from Joburg, several hundred people gathered to meet the mission plane and to welcome Mark. Most villagers were convinced that he would surely die from the snake bite, so when they saw Mark get out of the plane, walking unassisted on his own two feet, they believed that they were seeing a miracle by the Great Physician—and they may have.

Treating snake bites and other animal-inflicted injuries weren't the only unusual duties of the African bush doctor. Because Mukinge was the only hospital in the district, it was required of the doctors there to perform the postmortem exams as ordered by the local magistrate. These were required when anyone died under unusual circumstances, and particularly when there was concern about foul play. These exams were always inconvenient to fit into an already busy schedule, but they did force the doctors to get involved with all of the murder cases and the bizarre causes of death.

The worst possible scenario was when the police would exhume a badly decomposed body that had been buried for a long time, and expect that a doctor could tell them whether poisoning had been the cause of death.

What usually happened was that a younger person died without having a known significant sickness. The local family would go ahead with the arrangements and bury the deceased.

In the next week or so, other relatives would gather from out of town to grieve with their family, and then would convince the local family members that their relative certainly must have been

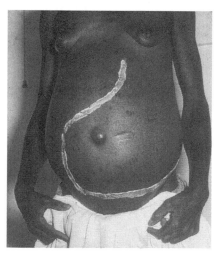

*Many tropical diseases produce massive spleens.*

poisoned by some enemy. A postmortem would be required to prove this. (This made no sense at all since the local poisons are all from plant sources and are usually indetectable after a short period. Furthermore, Zambia had no toxicologist, so it would be of no value to send blood and stomach contents to the medical center even from a fresh cadaver, let alone one that was many days or weeks old.) The postmortem changes in the tropics are so rapid that it is imperative to keep the bodies in a refrigerated compartment in the morgue immediately after death if meaningful conclusions are to be drawn.

"I was assisted by a medical student from Oxford while examining an exhumed body," Jim recalled. He thought her evaluation of that task was quite fitting when she concluded, "That was the most disgusting thing I have ever done in my life!"

"It was always enjoyable to have medical students with me when I did postmortems," Jim said. One of the advantages was that Jim made them sew up the long incision, which gave them valuable experience in suturing and saved him some time since they could finish their job after he left.

Another reason Jim enjoyed the students was that it gave him an opportunity to demonstrate a phenomenon of rural Zambia. Cutting through the coronary arteries, Jim would show the young students how the arteries were thin, full bore, and totally pliable. "I assured them that their coronaries didn't look like that," Jim said. Grease and fat-laden foods such as burgers and fries are too expensive, not to mention unavailable to the rural Zambian.

Jim explained, "The coronaries of an aged Kaonde man look just like a child's, thin and supple, no hint at all of hardening or narrowing." As a result, Jim never saw a local person with a myocardial infarction, a heart attack.

Jim admitted that the rural Africans' way of life includes a lot of exercise—walking and manual labor. Their stress levels are also considerably lower than those of city dwellers. "But certainly the big factor is what they put in their mouths," Jim insisted.

His conclusion: atherosclerosis, the underlying cause of all heart attacks and most strokes, is totally preventable!

The English physician, Dr. Denis Burkitt (for whom Burkitt's Lymphoma was named), was known as the Fiber Man. He was an early advocate of eating foods in nature's packages. Mukinge was one of the early corresponding hospitals contributing to Dr. Burkitt's postage-stamp research on why the rural African was spared five diseases very common in the West.

Dr. Burkitt proved that fiber-depleted diets were closely associated with bowel cancer, appendicitis, diverticulitis, and gallstones.

Jim listed three more diseases common in Westerners but rare in rural Africa: hiatus hernia, diabetes, and deep venous thrombosis.

Jim was taught in medical school that fiber was too scratchy to give to someone with diverticulitis or other serious bowel complaints. "Dr. Burkitt convinced the rest of the world that fiber is good, not bad. That took quite a bit of doing to convince the medical establishment, with his African statistics, that the conventional wisdom was completely wrong," Jim said.

Jim reflected, "Dr. Burkitt was a godly man and one of my heroes. He placed no value on the glory and fame that drive so many researchers."

Jim stated:

Mukinge villagers routinely eat as much as fifty or sixty grams of fiber daily, most of it in the form of nshima (corn mush). Colon cancer was never confirmed in any of our patients.

Gallstones were a great oddity, rather hard to develop when there is so little lipid floating around in their blood or gut. The handful of acute appendicitis cases that came to us were invariably in people who had abandoned the typical rural diet.

Out of the thousands of women who came to our clinic each year, only four or five would present with breast cancer, rather than the one in nine statistic in American women. (The details of the differences between the Western diet and the rural African diet— plus the important role of fiber—are clearly described in Burkitt's book *Eat Right to Stay Healthy and Enjoy Life More*.)

The more Jim observed the healthy lifestyle of his patients, the more convinced he became that eating unhealthy food was displeasing to God—at least for him. Jim said, "When I would discuss with Westerners on furlough the 'light' that God had given me concerning a healthy diet, I would often get the response: 'Please keep your light to yourself.'" But to this day, Jim believes that Scripture makes it clear that believers should treat their bodies as "temples of the Holy Spirit" (1 Cor. 6:19–20 NIV), honoring God with their bodies, which includes honoring God in what they eat.

# Chapter Twenty-two
## Marilynn in Mission

Meanwhile, Marilynn was glorifying God in her life in countless ways of her own. Her ministry embraced nursing, both practicing and teaching. She had a natural gift for languages, which she used in teaching the new missionaries to speak Kikaonde. Marilynn not only had the opportunity to introduce them to the complexities of the language, but also to pass on to them her love for the people and her respect for their culture. She also spent years teaching the older, illiterate Mukinge Church ladies how to read and write in their own language, as well as leading them in Bible studies.

In the 1960s, the government of newly independent Zambia began recruiting young, strong, and jobless teenagers in what was called Rural Reconstruction Centers (RRC). The early emphasis in the military-like camps was on agriculture—much like the old Civil Conservation Corps (CCC) in the U.S. in the 1930s. It was an opportunity for God's work that was soon to become quite significant.

Marilynn related in a prayer letter from those early days: "The RRC camp nearest us is at Kafumfula, about thirty miles from Mukinge, where there were 120 plus teenagers, away from home and wondering what life is all about. Enter the gospel."

The entry into the camp was provided by one of the RRC youth who used to sing in Marilynn's choir at Mukinge. The lad told Marilynn that he and a few other Christians at the camp were trying to meet together, but they really didn't know what they were doing. He asked Marilynn, "please come and help."

Soon after that, Marilynn rounded up a preacher and a singing group and held a meeting at the camp. Fourteen lads and the camp director responded to the gospel message.

A few weeks later, the Mukinge preacher who had gone on the first visit came to Marilynn and referred to the new believers by asking, "Is it right to give birth to a baby, and then just leave it to die without feeding it?"

Marilynn already felt guilty about not following up on the new believers, but the RRC was built in the middle of nowhere and the last ten miles of "un-road" was an endurance contest for both car and driver—a trip that couldn't fit easily into anyone's weekly schedule.

"What a tug at the heart! But all I could promise at that point was to pray for them every day and try to find a way to visit them regularly," Marilynn said.

Much to Marilynn's delight, in her later visits she found a "thriving little church (about twenty-five to thirty boys) with logs for pews and an anthill for the podium." The little congregation met on Mondays for choir practice, Wednesdays for prayer, Fridays for Bible study, and Sundays for worship.

A few months later, the Lord met the group's need for a mature Bible teacher in a most unusual way—and involving Marilynn.

One day as she was driving down the road near the hospital, Marilynn looked down a hill and saw the RRC tractor overturned—the wheels still turning, the engine still running, and a pair of arms waving frantically underneath.

She quickly ran down to help but she admitted, "I was so clueless that I didn't even know how to turn the thing off." Eventually, help came and they got the injured man out from under the tractor.

He spent two months recovering at Mukinge Hospital, where he was fed nshima and large daily doses of Scripture.

The man had made a commitment to follow Christ ten years ago, but in the meantime, had gone the way of the world. His near-death experience, however, caused him to see the error of his ways, and he repented of his sins. During his long stay at the hospital, he made a complete spiritual recovery, becoming a strong believer.

The day before the patient left the hospital, Marilynn learned that he was actually the agricultural instructor at the camp. The Lord had answered the boys' prayer for a mature helper with a man who, like Jonah, had been running away from his Creator. The Lord had to use a big fish to get Jonah's attention; an overturned tractor did the job for the agricultural director. He returned to Kafumfula, zealous to minister to the young believers at the RRC camp.

# Marilynn in Mission

When the Foulkes family first arrived in Mukinge, the churches were made up mostly of older people. Marilynn's love for music led her to work with Paul Makai, a gifted young musician and the headmaster of a local primary school. Paul, who is now the bishop over the eight hundred churches that are part of the Evangelical Church of Zambia, also had a heart to reach out to the young. Together, Marilynn and Paul planted and nurtured choirs, developing indigenous worship music that helped to bring a flood of youth into the area churches.

Today, most of the churches have two or three choirs, and at the big annual church conference, close to half of the attendees are young people who come with their local church choirs. The choirs brought the young people back to church, and the bi-weekly choir practices became the major youth event for the rural churches.

Marilynn was never happier than when she was surrounded by fifteen or twenty choirs at the workshops she organized. Often, their songs of praise would lift them into the presence of God and they would sing all night long!

Several of the songs were ones that Marilynn had translated from English into Kikaonde, and others were hymns that Paul had composed. She collected one hundred new Kikaonde hymns, and made them into a supplementary hymnbook. As a gifted pianist,

*A young Paul Makai (on right) and Maluben Kashale. At this time, Paul was composing hymns in the vernacular and travelling with Marilynn to establish choirs all over Zambia. Paul was the best man in our wedding at Mukinge, and he is now the bishop over the eight hundred churches of the Evangelical Church in Zambia.*

*Getting to the TEE class at Nyoka in the rainy season was always a challenge.*

Marilynn was asked to play at the meetings attended by overflow crowds during the Billy Graham crusade in Zambia in 1959.

But even before Paul's arrival at Kasempa, Marilynn was devoted to leading a choir with the student nurses and helping with the music at Mukinge Church from time to time. Music was an instrument of grace that opened doors for her on many levels to share the good news. A student of the Scriptures, she was an evangelical agent of change in the lives of many.

In a missionary letter penned en route to Zambia as the family returned from a stateside furlough, Marilynn wrote:

> *As we see it from here, our most important job as missionaries in the next few years is to plant the Word deeply into the hearts of the people. That is the only thing that can keep any Christian walking straight. We feel that Theological Education by Extension (TEE) is one really good answer to the question: How can this be accomplished?*

The purpose of the seminary extension program was to bring systematic Scripture education to many Christians, instead of just the traditional few who could afford the time and money to go off to a resident Bible school. TEE required the students to study the self-instructing lessons at home for two hours a day. On first arrival at the class, the supervisor required them to take an exam on the work of the week. After the weekly quiz, the next two hours were spent in discussing the material and applying it. At the end of the course the students wrote a two-hour comprehensive exam about all the material covered in the ten-week course.

But the TEE program in the Kasempa district needed a leader who could give at least twelve hours a week to supervise all the classes being taught in the district. Despite the heavy load he was carrying at the hospital, Jim agreed to be the TEE director—only after Marilynn agreed to grade all of the exam papers, and his associate, Dr. Bob Wenninger, kindly offered to shoulder the extra medical duties.

The first TEE graduation thrilled both Marilynn and Jim, who handed out the diplomas to the seventeen graduates who had successfully completed the three-year program from the three

*A happy day to be able to present TEE completion certificates to Willem Berendsen for thirty-four courses (three courses a year for eleven years) and Joshua Mumpande for twenty-four courses (three courses a year for eight years)—a great example of faithfulness. Willem has completed more courses than any other TEE student in Africa.*

centers. The graduation ceremony was held at the annual church conference attended by three thousand people.

Marilynn and Jim were further encouraged when they learned that four men from their TEE class were going on to resident Bible school to complete their full diplomas, and three more were going to enroll the next year. The graduation served as a stimulus to the other eighty TEE students in the district to persevere and finish their courses.

But little did the Foulkes family know it was on a countdown that would alter their lives.

# Chapter Twenty-three
## Tragedy and Comfort

For a period of time, Jim found himself praying for two miracles: healing for his wife *and* his daughter. Both were seriously ill. Jill, then aged fifteen, became ill in August 1976, with swollen ankles and fatigue. Soon after that, a lump in Marilynn's breast, which had been an ongoing concern for several months, started to grow larger and was joined by swollen lymph nodes underneath her armpit.

Jim took her to see the chief surgeon at the Kitwe Central Mine hospital in the copperbelt. After his examination, his statement shook Jim's composure. "I want you both on a plane tomorrow either heading to South Africa or America!"

Jim recalled, "It was like a death sentence, and I was so over come that even the next day I didn't say a word all during our drive to the capital." In Capetown, a biopsy confirmed cancer. A mastectomy was followed by a long course of triple chemotherapy.

Jill's diagnosis was more of a mystery. She began to experience a low-grade fever, developed an enlarged liver and, later, an enlarged spleen. Although she did not develop the typical yellow jaundice, infectious hepatitis, a viral disease commonly encountered among third-world missionaries, was initially thought to be the most likely diagnosis.

Improving somewhat, Jill returned to boarding school in Kenya, only to be sent back to Zambia when her condition did not turn the corner towards expected recovery.

Marilynn vividly described her personal battle with cancer in a prayer letter written soon after the Christmas holidays:

*During these months, I have the distinct sense of traveling down a straight path, a little rocky, but not frightening, because I was being led by the hand of Jesus. One private prayer that I had, was that I might not bring shame upon the name of Christ, before others who did not know Him.*

# To Africa with Love

*I've known myself for a long time as a coward, and I was afraid that, in a pinch, that unfortunate character trait might surface, and mess things up. But God's love became so real and all-encompassing, that it was like a warm blanket which covered me right up to my neck, protecting me from all evil. Because of that, I didn't even have to be brave . . . "His banner over me is love."*

Marilynn's deep faith even enabled her to see some benefit in her situation.

*One wonderful compensation for having my wings clipped, is that I was at home all the time during the Christmas holidays. As far back as my kids can remember, their mommy has been busy with outside commitment during this family time. Instead, I got to spend the whole time with them, and it was sweet.*

After the holidays, Jill improved somewhat and was feeling strong enough to return to Kenya's Rift Valley Academy for the spring semester. Alas, her recovery was short lived. After another spell in the school infirmary, she was forced to return home.

She went for tests at the big hospital in Capetown, South Africa. The liver biopsy failed to confirm the hepatitis diagnosis, and the lab studies that went on for several weeks turned up no definitive diagnosis.

While in the Capetown hospital, Jill was chosen to be the star patient of "grand rounds." Doctors in training lined up to palpate her spleen, which had become enormous, filling half of her abdominal cavity.

Despite this test of her patience and the ordeal of numerous needles and tubes that went on for weeks on end, she ministered in her own way to doctors, nurses, and other patients. Jill made her own version of rounds, and especially liked to read passages from her well-worn Bible to the lonely elderly ladies, her immediate neighbors on the hospital ward.

After returning to Mukinge, Jill developed some new symptoms that raised the question of kala-azar, a parasitic disease that is extremely rare in Zambia, but endemic in a part of Kenya where Jill had spent some time. Her early response to treatment, along with serum samples sent to the Center for Disease Control and Prevention (CDC) in Atlanta, seemed to confirm the diagnosis.

Her raging fevers that often went to 105 degrees stopped. But within a week, some low-grade fever returned and she continued to deteriorate.

Jill relapsed with high fevers, and this time they did not go away with anti-infective medications. It soon became clear that Jill's illness was terminal. The final diagnosis was only made after her death: erythro-leukemia, a very rare form of leukemia that affects the red cells. She spent the last months of her life at home in Mukinge, mostly in bed; increasingly weak physically, though her spirit remained strong. Whenever her pain became unbearable, Jill would sing hymns, often of her own composition.

*Sweet Jill, two years before she died.*

Jill's bedroom began to resemble a hospital ward, with intravenous fluids running around the clock and a host of missionary nurses taking shifts to care for her. Not the least of these, of course, was her mother.

Another caretaker was Auntie Marge Harstine, a close friend from Ohio. She put it this way: "None of us caring for Jill during her last five weeks will ever be the same again; we all knew that we were caring for an angel." Jill prayed without ceasing that her illness would bring glory to God. Jim said, "Apart from that, her long, cruel illness had no meaning at all—not to her or to us."

One time during Jill's semi-comatose last few days on earth, she was stirred into consciousness, whispering that she had glimpses of heaven folding before her eyes. She started to sing the well-known hymn, "Just As I Am." Getting to the line "I come," she looked up with a beautiful smile and sang the words over and over. Jill so wanted to go and be with Jesus.

Her beatific vision, however, was quickly overshadowed by the realization that she was back in the world of intravenous lines and pain. It wasn't yet her time.

"Mommy, why did I have to come back here?" she asked Marilynn. "Why did Jesus call me, if He hadn't wanted me just then?"

The final call came the very next day; she died in her sleep. Jim said it all soon afterwards in a letter:

*Jill's tired, worn-out body could no longer contain that vibrant eternal spirit of hers, a spirit that would now be able to sing a fresh song of joy, without pain, in the very presence of Jesus. Jill, our own little Hobbit (she loved to read Tolkien's* The Lord of the Rings), *had carried her ring to the end, through unbelievable odds.*

The famous African bush telegraph also works in the mission compound, and before long, some of the student nurses, about forty in number, gathered at the Foulkes residence, which was within a few yards of the hospital. Between their sobbing, they softly sang the old hymn "Rock of Ages."

Soon, a train of bare feet was shuffling into and out of the living room, as the local Zambians paid their respects to the grieving family. Said Jim, soon afterwards: "The very people we were sent here to minister to were ministering to us! We received much comfort from their open arms. It was like a loving touch from the Lord."

Marilynn was in regular touch with a pastor friend, Don Miller of Hope Church in St. Louis, Missouri. She shared some of her deepest feeling with him in a letter:

*In such a case as Jill's, it's hard to know how to interpret scriptural promises such as "the prayer of faith will save the sick," and "whatsoever things ye desire when you pray, believe that ye receive them, and ye shall have them." Many had prayed for Jill, completely convinced that she would be healed; praying in faith, even "up to the minute she took her last breath." Jill's death was a potential blow to their faith. Some were asking: "So next time, how should we pray? How can we pray again with believing faith?"*

*For me personally, it wasn't a problem, because I was at such a complete loss as how to pray for "my baby." I had a feeling deep down in my heart that she would be taken. As I cared for her, day after day, these words kept ringing in my mind: ". . . of whom the world was not worthy." All through those months, I was just asking for His presence with us all.*

# Tragedy and Comfort

*Strength to endure, with patience. When the going got tough, I just gave myself to the Spirit, and asked Him to pray for me, because I didn't know what to say!*

All along, Jill had prayed that her life, including her illness, would somehow glorify God. Beyond her life, illness, and death, that prayer continues to be answered. Her sister, Gwen, stood up at the funeral, sharing Scripture from the Old Testament: "Give to the Lord the glory due His name, bring an offering and come before Him" (Ps. 96:8). Gwen said that the one offering that Jill's family could bring was a fresh commitment of their lives to God. She challenged others listening, especially the young people present, to do the same.

A government official showed up at the graveside service totally unprepared for what he would experience. After listening to those who shared, he rose solemnly to add a few words of his own:

> We non-Christians do not know how to die. We count death as a terrible, final loss, but you Christians are different. I say to you other non-Christians here today, if any preacher comes to your house, you listen to him, because the words of God are true!

Jill's story touched others even farther afield. A youth magazine, published by Back to the Bible Ministries, ran an article: "Death of an M.K.", which drew widespread response from readers of all ages. The M.K. (missionary kid) story was reprinted again since more reprints were requested for that story than any other that year.

The Foulkeses heard from strangers throughout the world telling how Jill's story had blessed them. Many declared how the story had helped them understand something more about God's purposes in death. Some had harbored bitter feelings against the Lord, and the article helped to bring those out into His healing light.

Jill's sister, Terrie, shared the article with a college friend who, after reading it, sobbed with tears of conviction, soon to be replaced by tears of joy, as the friend gave her life to Christ.

Jim said years later, "There's no way of knowing for sure, but perhaps Jill's short sixteen-year life touched more people in her death than would have been possible if she had lived long. Though short in years, Jill lived the precious gift of her life fully and deeply. Today she leaves a spiritual legacy that will stand for eternity."

## To Africa with Love

Auntie Joy Warner, the godly physical therapist, wrote this poem while grieving deeply over Jill's death:

> He lent her to a family
> to live on earth awhile.
> She left her place in heaven
> and secretly she came
> to live, as no other angel has,
> among the sons of men.
> Her hair was jet
> her eyelashes as others never seen
> her lips of dying rose
> worn only by a queen.
> Her words were few while here on earth
> she spoke mostly with her smile.
> Because within her eyes
> she told of heavenly secrets known only in the skies.
> Her walk here, gentle, thoughtful, quiet
> a touch of the divine
> for He lent her to us here on earth
> for just a little time.
> And now she has returned again
> the road from whence she came.
> Oh do not weep my child, my son.
> For you in faithfulness have won
> My wish—the glory of my Name
> I only lent her.

Shortly after Jill's death, Jim and Marilynn were invited to join some friends attending a conference three hundred miles west of Mukinge. At first, they were hesitant about taking their mood of intense grief into a group of joyful Christians; and, arriving at the conference, they were surprised to learn that the planned focus for the week was to be "Praise to God."

Jim and Marilynn looked at each other and wondered if they had come to the wrong place. What, in human terms, did they have to be thankful for? What reason to praise Him, having already lost two of their family members to an early grave, and now circumstances were pointing toward yet another premature death? As Jim noted, "I could readily confess that most of my praise to God had occurred when good things were happening, not when bad things hit."

But as the conference week gradually unfolded, the love and ministry of their fellow believers slowly brought about a transformation in the hearts of the hurting couple. They worshipped God, even if through their tears, as the Holy One.

Beams of light broke through into their dark tunnel of sadness, and after several days, they could join in, hearts and minds, with the worship songs. By the end of it all, they had learned an important faith principle: Praising God in adversity is the true path to His peace. This was a truth they would treasure and lean on in the difficult days still to come.

Jim recalled:

> God had given us an awesome gift during the week and we were now at peace about Marilynn's future. It was a peace that never left us. The perfect peace of the Lord is not bound by circumstances. To paraphrase some verses from John 14: My peace I give unto you, not as the world gives . . . so do not be afraid.

At the end of the week, Jim and Marilynn asked the elders to anoint her, as prescribed in Scripture, "in the name of the Lord" (James 5:14–15). The two covenanted that they would spend some time together each day simply worshipping God together.

Jim said, "In the days to come, our feeble efforts to be faithful to that new leading bore fruit in our lives."

But for Marilynn, time was running out.

# ChapterTwenty-four
## A Faithful End to the Good Fight

**M**arilynn was a most courageous person. She bravely faced her own grave prognosis while still grieving over the death of her dear daughter Jill. Her main concern was that she would fall short of the mission God had given her, in whatever time she had left.

She wrote Pastor Miller: "I want to finish the work God has for me to do, so I will not be ashamed when I see Him." It would only be human for her to want to live long enough to see her three daughters wed, and even to hold some of her grandchildren. But that was not to be.

Jim said:

> While we were praying for Marilynn's healing, looking forward to the glory that Christ would receive for healing her, she was being controlled by the same desire Paul expressed in his letter to the Philippian Christians that: "Christ shall be magnified in my body, whether it be by life or by death" (Phil. 1:20).

> Without question, Marilynn's ministry was accelerated in the last five years of her life. She was on a countdown that we were unaware of at the time. The impact of her loving, spirit-filled life was far beyond natural explanation.

Sadly, the cancer was beginning to take its toll. In the last year of her life, Marilynn no longer had the stamina to drive over the long bumpy roads to teach her TEE classes. She added other classes, however, that were located nearer home.

Teaching the Word became Marilynn's highest priority. She had always found a great joy in discipling young Christians, especially those that she had led to accepting Jesus. She spent many nights praying for her wayward sons.

Alas, her life at Mukinge came to an abrupt end that fateful September. Another recurrence of cancer made it necessary for Marilynn, Jim, and Gwen to make an extended trip down to Capetown, where she could be treated at the huge regional hospital.

She started radiotherapy under the care of her doctors, and seemed to be holding her own physically. Jim felt comfortable returning to his duties at Mukinge for the time being, while Marilynn continued to show slight improvement. Gwennie stayed on in Capetown with her mommy, the twosome staying at the mission guest house run by fellow missionaries, Zip and Len Glass.

While there, Marilynn agreed to speak at a large Baptist Women's Conference, which included women from churches all over the Cape Province, there at the southern tip of South Africa. She had become so fatigued just before the conference, however, that she had asked that her name be removed from the speakers' roster. Some days later, though, she became convinced that the Lord really wanted her to go ahead with it, and to present her testimony. As always in these matters, she obeyed the Lord's prompting.

Jim recalled, "I later heard from many people what a great impact her testimony had, coming from an obviously dying woman who was too weak to even stand up at the podium."

Jim was notified that he should return to Capetown, since it was becoming more and more evident that Marilynn was dying. The cancer had invaded her spine at several levels, causing excruciating pain with the slightest movement of her legs. Arriving soon afterwards, Jim went straight to visit her in the hospital and realized immediately that she did not have long to live.

"She wanted to have a chance to say good-bye to Jackie and Terrie, as well as her many Mukinge friends," Jim remembered. So the next day, he made arrangements with the Red Cross of South Africa to fly Marilynn to the Botswana border, where the mission plane could then take her on to the mission in Zambia, a total distance of twenty-five hundred miles.

Unfortunately, when the day set for the flight arrived, Marilynn began having bouts of uncontrolled bleeding. The cancer had invaded her bone marrow, and she was no longer producing the normal anticoagulant factors. "She would not have survived the flight, and she needed fresh whole blood immediately. So the flight was cancelled," Jim said.

# A Faithful End to the Good Fight

Jim got an urgent call at the guest house early on Sunday morning. It was the nurse at the hospital, reporting that Marilynn had suffered a massive brain hemorrhage. She told Jim that if he wanted to see his wife alive, he should come over to the hospital immediately. Marilynn was unconscious and breathing unevenly when Jim entered the hospital room. It was plain to the husband-physician that his beloved wife was close to the end of her suffering.

November 20, 1977, was Coronation Day for Marilynn Hall Foulkes. She had fought the good fight. She had kept the faith. She had completed her *kikonkwanyi* (her assigned task).

Jim sat at her bedside, with her hand cupped in his, tears streaming down his face. The triumphant strains of the "Hallelujah Chorus" from Handel's *Messiah*, playing on his tape recorder, filled the hospital room. For one who loved music such as Marilynn, it was as if the Holy Spirit Himself had scripted her very death.

"If my ears had not been so dull, I'm sure that I could have heard the glorious angelic hallelujahs welcome her into the presence of the Lord that she loved and served so well," Jim said.

When Jim went over to tell the head nurse that Marilynn had died, she asked him: "Who do you want me to call?" Then it hit him—there was nobody to call. His fellow missionary, Len Glass, was preaching across the Cape that Sunday morning. Gwennie was attending a youth event up the coast and would be gone for the weekend.

He longed for the company of their many good friends back in Mukinge, who would have loved to throw their arms around him. But at that moment, they were nearly three thousand miles away. He was all alone.

As never before in his life, Jim felt totally abandoned. Where was God at that moment of his greatest need?

A student nurse, whom he had gotten to know as a believer, saw his plight. She asked, "Doctor, would you like me to pray for you?"

Jim said:

We kneeled down beside my dead wife, and she started to pray. I have no memory of any of her words. But I will never forget the beauty and power of the presence of the Lord, as He filled the room and my empty, grieving heart. It was perhaps the most

189

glorious experience of my life. That was the covenant that Marilynn and I had made many years before with the Lord. He said: "I want you to go and leave your family and friends and culture behind, but I will be with you to the very end," and we proved His promise true.

A pastor friend from Zambia, Rev. Graham Ingram, who was now attached to a church in Capetown, agreed to do the memorial service at the large Kenilworth Baptist Church. Marilynn had always looked forward to Graham's daily visits to her in the hospital, since he always came with a fresh word from the Lord that greatly encouraged her. Gwennie and Marilynn had made many friends at the Kenilworth church during their stays with the Glass family.

Graham's opening remarks were from the book of Revelation: "Blessed are the dead, who die in the Lord" (Rev. 14:13). He asked the rhetorical question: "How could it be called a blessing, to see a mother with young children struck down in her prime?" He went on to describe Marilynn's many gifts, and asked again how it could be called blessed for the Zambian church to lose such a valuable missionary?

The answer, said Graham, comes in those last three words—*in the Lord*. That change in perspective completely alters the seeming tragedy into something blessed. The Spirit further comments in the next sentence: "Blessed indeed! Now they can rest for ever and ever after their work, because their good deeds go with them."

Marilynn's good deeds stayed with all of those who knew her. The loveliness of Christ that she transmitted to everyone throughout her life remained like the sweet fragrance of a rose that fills the room even after the actual flower is removed.

Another memorial service was held at the Mukinge Church. Jim was happy when his brother Dick arrived from Costa Rica, just three hours before the service started. The crowd filled the church to overflowing, and a loudspeaker was set up for the several hundred people that were standing three-deep outside the building.

Jim knew that Marilynn would not want praises heaped upon her head. Instead, she would want the name of Christ to be held up and glorified. However, it did seem fitting for several of her friends to relate how Marilynn's life had brought them closer to Jesus.

# A Faithful End to the Good Fight

Marge Harstine, their neighbor on the mission compound, told how God had used Marilynn to call her to Mukinge some eighteen years before, and how Marilynn's life had such a profound influence on her own walk with the Lord.

The Zambian high schooler named Batty, who lived with the Foulkes family, was terribly shaken. Marilynn had been the only stable and loving influence in his life. Nevertheless, the young man was able to control his shattered emotions long enough to recount the words of comfort that she had left with him on the night before her last trip to Capetown.

One of the church leaders paid tribute to her as a truly color-blind missionary, whose teaching and example would be discussed around campfires for many years to come.

The choir that Marilynn had founded and trained, sang with tear-filled eyes.

But we'll let Marilynn herself have the last word, as she wrote in a prayer letter shortly before her illness:

*My personal testimony for the new year is [appreciating] a deep sense of God's supremacy over everything that concerns me and mine. Without Him, there is nothing: a vacuum. In the words of a Kaonde song that our choir sings:*

> Jesus is the owner of my life
> He is my daily conversation
> Without Him I can't breathe
> I can only die.

*That's about it. May God help us all to proclaim that message faithfully in our generation.*

In the final analysis, that's exactly what she did.

# Chapter Twenty-five
## A Time to Mourn

Jim had suddenly become reacquainted with grief. His daughter Jill had died only three months before Marilynn; and his little David's death still evoked fresh memories from time to time, even though the toddler had been dead many years.

The death of his children had been devastating. But with his wife alongside him, he had an anchor. They could cling to one another when the deep waves of grief threatened to engulf them. They could comfort and console one another, and that made the pain almost bearable. They could pray together to the God of all comfort.

Marilynn's death, however, wounded him to the core of his being. It was different from anything else he had experienced, and it felt like an open sore that did not want to heal. His partner-for-life had been ripped away from him. When men and women get married, the two become one. The marriage bond, in contrast with the child-parent relationship, is until death us do part. So, when one is taken by death, the one left behind becomes *less* than one; it leaves the survivor diminished, less than whole.

Jim found that his intense grief mimicked depression in many ways. He had the same characteristic loss of appetite and the same loss of interest in the mundane things of life. He started losing weight. The lack of sleep began to cause dark circles to form under his eyes. Jim's friends became concerned for his health.

Meanwhile, his girls were having to walk the same road in learning to live without their loved ones. And they were trying their best to comfort their father.

Jim, himself, was learning that making the effort to praise God during adversity is the best way to dispel grief. Praise is simply incompatible with self-pity. The two cannot abide together. Discouragement, bitterness, and all the other temptations that beset the bereaved one are robbed of their power to do harm.

In the words of Catherine Marshall: "When we praise . . . perspective comes. When we have turned our back on the problem, and are looking steadily at God, we are acting out our belief in the character of God, His goodness and His love."

Jim noted, "The people who can help most are the ones who have been through the deep waters, and are faithfully passing on to others the comfort and insights given to them by the God of all comfort." Now Jim desperately needed that comfort. The many days that he spent in the valley of the shadow of death were, as he put it: "anointed with tears, a long night of weeping."

It was the wisdom on a plaque, sent to him by fellow missionary Elwanda Fields, that spoke to his heart at the very deepest level. He hung this plaque on his office wall, looking at it many times throughout the day. It read: "Your heavenly father is too good to be unkind, and too wise to make a mistake."

Says Jim of that time:

> I knew my God well enough to know that, deep down inside, these words held true. When circumstances were shouting out that God had let me down, I knew that I needed the Lord's help to live out what I actually believed. His grace was indeed sufficient.

> I sincerely hoped that He would answer the prayers of many for Marilynn's healing. Submitting to His sovereign will to heal Marilynn in death was truly difficult, but I knew that the two great enemies of the grieving Christian are self-pity and anger toward God.

> In this process, I was helped by the wisdom contained in a C. S. Lewis essay [*God in the Dock*], in which he asks: "Who are we to put God Almighty in the dock, in the seat of the accused, and then point our finger in his face?"

During the sleepless hours of the night, Jim would often sing quietly: "Thou art my God, and I will praise you/Thou art my God, and I will exalt you . . ." (Ps. 118:28). Then God, the Comforter, would come, bringing peace to his troubled mind, and he would fall into some semblance of sleep.

# A Time to Mourn

Looking back, as he often did then, Jim's thoughts would gravitate towards the good times he had shared with Marilynn and the girls. Those whirlwind holidays they all enjoyed, piling into the big orange truck, rolling through the game parks, feeling the ground shake under the thundering hooves of stampeding buffalo and wildebeest herds; hearing something go bump in the night and tumbling out of bed to see a rhino materialize in the beam of his flashlight, the great beast with its horn tangled in the guy ropes of the family tent, and feeling sad when the rain finally washed its muddy silhouette from the side of the tent a year later. He remembered experiences like camping on the white sand dunes north of Beira, down on the Indian Ocean, walking on the coral reef; watching the crocodiles on the banks of the Nile in Uganda, singing songs, and telling stories around the many campfires they had shared together.

Now, all those moments of his life with Marilynn were relegated to mere memory, and the stark reality was that there would be no more additions to their journey together, not this side of heaven.

Jim found that singing worship songs with his girls, usually accompanied by Gwennie's guitar, had become a great balm of Gilead, as it helped to jumpstart the healing process. He recalled:

We praised God, while embracing each other with assuring hugs and warm hearts.

> Fear not, for I have redeemed you, I have called you by name,
> When you pass through the waters, I will be with you
> And when you pass through the rivers, they will not sweep
>   over you,
> When you walk through the fire, you will not be burned.

This verse from Isaiah 43, put to music, was a frequent solace to our hearts. We sang it often, both in private and with friends. For us, these promises were a special gift from the Father.

The word of God was paramount in ministry to Jim and his daughters: "We were given a heightened sensitivity to the Book. We felt God's Spirit alongside us many times each day."

Jim's brother Dick took a leave of absence from his missionary duties in Costa Rica to stay with the family for several weeks and to help ease the burden of their grief. It seems that some of Jim's Zambian friends had another role in mind for his brother, though— they asked Jim when his brother would be returning to choose a replacement wife for him! In the local culture, three months is considered a reasonable amount of time for a widower to wait before marrying again.

"They were concerned that my brother had not yet performed his duty." Jim politely thanked them for their concern, with the prompt assurance that remarriage was the farthest thing from his thoughts at that time.

He returned to work full time at the hospital, noting that getting involved with other people's problems would be good grief therapy for himself. Jim shared Scriptures, especially from Job and from 2 Corinthians chapter four, with dying patients and their grieving relatives. In this way, he was able to pass on to others the comfort of the Father, wherewith he had been comforted himself.

"It is a great gift, as a doctor, when from your heart, you can cry with those who cry and rejoice with those who rejoice. Especially when you have been there yourself!" Jim observed.

He also had the solace of his three daughters, who had stayed home until the new year, after which Terrie returned to college in the U.S., and Jackie returned to high school in Kenya. Gwennie, then between high school and college, stayed home with her father until it was time for the two of them to return to the United States that summer for their scheduled furlough. The other two girls were then reunited with their father before they all returned to their studies in the fall semester.

A letter that Jim wrote from Lima towards the end of that year reveals how broken pieces of his heart were gradually being put back together again by a loving, compassionate Savior. It was the end of his first furlough without Marilynn. The deaths of his daughter and his wife were still in the back of his mind, but the letter is full of praise to the Lord from a heart still healing.

Dear ones, 1978 has been a year of adjustments. The greatest adjustment has been learning to live without Marilynn and Jill. As

# A Time to Mourn

C. S. Lewis described it so well, the loss of a spouse is similar to amputation . . . first there's the shock, then the pain, and then the long process of learning to live without the missing part. I thank God for all the resources we have in Jesus, that have helped us through this lonely time. It has been wonderful to experience the continued balm we get from walking daily in the word of God. Singing the Scriptures, either accompanied by Gwennie's guitar or by praise tapes, has become a precious part of our day, and it is still our unvarying experience that putting on the cloak of praise dispels the spirit of heaviness (Isa. 61:3).

As long as we remain (continuously abide) in the Vine, the fresh sap keeps flowing and fruit is produced. It was a new insight for me recently to realize that God is responsible not only for producing the fruit, but also for picking it. *Our* only function is to keep plugged in, and to give Him the glory.

The theme of my furlough ministry was just to keep sharing with people the lessons He has been teaching me. I did not have the liberty to wander far from the themes of:

> Praising God in adversity,
> Passing on His comfort to others, and
> Allowing God to demonstrate His strength in weakness.

We will be heading for Sarasota, (Florida), to spend the third week in December with Mother and Dad Hall, and then we'll fly to Costa Rica to spend Christmas with my brother Dick and his family.

In the wonderful love of Jesus,<br>
Jim

It seemed so strange to sign his letter simply "Jim," since for the last twenty-two years, it had always been "Jim and Marilynn."

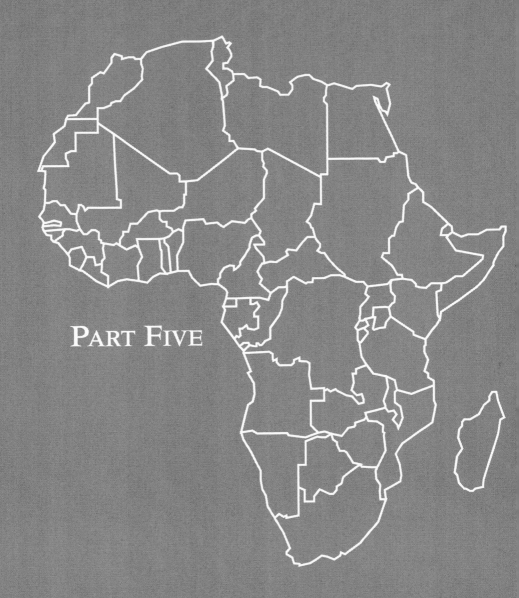

PART FIVE

# Chapter Twenty-six
## Martha

J im had no desire to remarry at the time. In fact, it seemed inappropriate to even consider the possibility. He was still weeping over the painful separation from Marilynn, not to mention making noble efforts to keep his family together. After the elder girls left for college, Jim and Jackie had to fend for themselves.

Jim said, "Jesus had already proven to me that His love was all I needed, and I knew that I could live the rest of my life supported only by Him."

But God had other plans. Jim began getting signals from God that He was going to give him Martha as his wife. Martha Penner was a missionary nurse from Canada who had worked at the hospital with Jim for several years. Jim later joked they had always been close; after all, Martha lived next door—only forty feet away!

Their romantic relationship started with an exchange of smiles; the smiles grew into friendship. He remembered, "When the signals kept coming, I began to accept that they were from above and that I should accept God's good gift with gladness."

Many months passed before he said anything to Martha. Living in a veritable fish bowl on a mission station, he had to be careful not to show publicly or privately that he cared for Martha.

It was only when they were on a KLM flight thirty thousand feet in the air going from Nairobi to Amsterdam—when his heart was *really* fluttering—that he worked up enough courage to even broach the subject of love and marriage. (Jim was on his way to London to attend a mission doctor's refresher course. Martha was visiting a mutual friend, Dorothy Haile, former headmistress of Mukinge Girl's Secondary School.)

The flight was packed, and Jim and Martha were sitting in the middle of the seven-passenger middle section of the 747, completely surrounded by people. But Jim had been practicing during a near sleepless night what he would say to Martha. He was not about to let potential eavesdroppers prevent him from declaring his love. Once the plane got off the ground, he didn't waste a lot of time before delivering his carefully rehearsed proposal.

Jim laughed, "I guess my thought was that I had better get it over with—for better or worse. Martha had picked up on a lot of cues during the weeks before we left Mukinge, and knew that I was in love with her. But somehow I thought that my confession of love for her would be a surprise."

Jim was so intent in expressing his love for Martha and his hope that she would be willing to become Mrs. Foulkes, that he initially forgot to ask if she would marry him . . . instead plunging headlong into a discussion of Martha's views on childbearing, and whether that was on her list of priorities.

"I was just as nervous as a proposing twenty-year-old, until I found that she also loved me and was willing to marry me," Jim said.

Martha speaks softly and laughs often, but never loudly—in contrast to Jim. Martha grew up in a Mennonite community close to Winnipeg. Following Bible school and nurses' training, she worked for a number of years in a hospital in Brantford, Ontario, before fulfilling her missionary calling in Mukinge.

Martha arrive at Mukinge in 1971, and immediately became

*Senior nursing students writing the national final exam that determines their futures. For many years, 100 percent of Mukinge's students passed.*

*Martha (far left) with a class of graduating super nurses and Doraine Ross (far right) at graduation, circa 1972. There are now more than six hundred graduates working all over Zambia.*

involved in the nurses' training school. For most of the time she had the responsibility of being the "principal tutor," the director of the Mukinge Enrolled Nursing School. The school has graduated hundreds of nurses who have since scattered across Zambia to serve in various government and mission hospitals, in addition to public health centers, to help meet the dire need for health-care workers.

The senior finalists at all nurses' training schools throughout Zambia were required to take a comprehensive final exam on the same day. The students lived in dread for the next couple of months while awaiting the test results. The test grades were sent to Martha, as the tutor in charge, who then called the finalists together to announce the results. The tension was always palpable.

One year, Martha had barely gotten the words "you have all passed" out of her mouth, before they stormed her, screaming and dancing—and knocking the poor tutor flat on her back! She quickly learned to always do a quick sidestep after releasing the results to escape the human avalanche of happy, exuberant students.

Martha's involvement with the students did not end with

graduation. It was a great joy for her to keep in contact with her graduates as they served faithfully all over Zambia. One of her grads, appropriately named Faith Liyena, was called into a ministry serving AIDS orphans, after nursing at Mukinge for two years. From very small beginnings, the Faith Orphans Foundation grew, and is now caring for more than three thousand AIDS orphans.

On the day of Jim and Martha's wedding, the sun was bright and shining, as if nature itself was decked out to enjoy the nuptial activities. The wedding was a strange blend of cultures, races, and nationalities. Paul Makai, Jim's close Zambian friend who had worked with Marilynn in her music ministry, was the best man. The three Foulkes sisters—Terrie, Jackie, and Gwen—were the bridesmaids. On behalf of Martha's father, John Penner, a dear friend dating back to college days, Gray Watson, gave away the bride. A women's choir traveled two hundred miles to attend, and sang wedding songs in the local language.

Keith Frew, another close friend and fellow missionary, led the service. A Zambian brother, Kashima Shayama, gave a word of encouragement and exhortation in the local language. The three bridesmaids sang a praise song, thanking the Lord for His greatness and

*The wedding reception following the ceremony. One thousand people gathered for the feast.*

*Jim and Martha's second wedding reception was held in the airplane hangar and had a western atmosphere. Daughters Terrie, Jackie, and Gwen feted them with a song of Gwen's composition.*

faithfulness. A choir of student nurses (whom Martha had tutored) concluded the singing with a moving rendition of the Doxology.

Once outside the church, local custom demands that the wedding party slowly walk the quarter mile to the place where the feast had been prepared. The wedding party was accompanied by the one thousand people coming to the feast.

The dust kicked up by the feet of the marchers mingled with the black soot floating down from a fresh grass fire on Mukinge Hill, rendering Martha's lovely white gown to a state of being permanently discolored. But the serene Martha—now Mrs. Foulkes—did not let that discordant note spoil the party. That evening, 120 missionaries and Zambian church people from many parts of the country gathered in an airplane hangar for the reception and celebrated in the American style with a wedding cake and all the trimmings.

As Jim mused on the goodness of God while looking at his happy, beaming bride, Isaiah 62:5 kept coming to mind: "And as the bridegroom rejoiceth over the bride, so shall thy God rejoice over thee."

Joy unbounded had replaced sadness and grief in his heart. The wheel had made a complete turn. He had a new helpmate; they could go hand-in-hand into the future. And he found that he could even worship God in the midst of a crowded wedding feast. His long, dark night of the soul was over.

# Chapter Twenty-seven
## All Healing Is God's

I f one asked Jim Foulkes if he believed marriages were made in heaven, he would undoubtedly answer, with a grin on his face, "I know of at least two."

It was now Jim and Martha. And with Christ as the center of their marriage, they were able to enter into a permanent relationship cemented by their deep love for one another.

Jim announced in his September 1980 prayer letter, "Martha was given special help from above, in being able to fulfill her role as a mother so well." The adjustment to her new role as wife and mother was easier for two reasons. She had worked closely with Jim in the hospital, and she had lived next door to the Foulkes family for many years. She could by no means be considered a stranger in the house.

Martha made a special effort to get close to Jackie, who at fourteen, was the youngest in the family. (Terrie and Gwen were stateside in college.) Jackie found it easy to love Martha. Jim was thrilled, of course, to see his two "girls" growing closer every day.

It didn't take long before Martha was exposed to a favorite Foulkes family event—a camping trip. All three girls made it home for the reunion. Terrie had just earned her degree in nursing at Clemson University, Gwennie had completed her second year at Columbia Bible College, and Jackie had squeezed eighteen weeks of correspondence work into seven weeks.

The family spent a week in what Jim casually referred to as his backyard. It is better known as the Kafue National Park, forty miles south of Mukinge. To Martha, it was exciting to view the abundance of wildlife that passed in review before their tent flaps.

Several elephants, however, came too close for the campers' comfort on two different nights, and they could not help remembering the recent killing of a Mukinge nurse by an elephant only six months earlier. Even Jungle Jim found the close encounter with the nosy jumbos a bit unnerving. It was a reminder that camping in Africa can have its risks as well as its exotic attractions.

At the request of his daughters, Jim drove the family three hundred miles through the game park to see the majestic Victoria Falls at Livingstone. The bridge to Zimbabwe had reopened, permitting the visitors to view the mile-wide thundering falls from both sides—the only way to capture the panoramic sweep of the mighty Zambezi River crashing down three hundred feet. The roar of the falls, along with the spectacle itself, makes a lasting impression on everyone who experiences it.

During the third week away from Mukinge, the family went back to the retreat site where Jim had been ministered to just after Jill and Marilynn had died. Many of the same people were there, giving him the opportunity to express his gratitude to them for teaching him a spiritual operating principle that he had made a part of his lifestyle—the giving of thanks in adversity to overcome grief.

*The Lufupa River that runs through the mission station was full of fish as it entered the nearby Kafue National Park. Here, Jackie displays her morning's catch. They didn't get much sleep that night since a pride of lions just across the river kept roaring at another pride behind them.*

"That was the key to our healing. As long as we kept praising, we were freed from self-pity or bitterness," Jim said.

The family took time each evening to sing around the campfire, accompanied by Gwennie's ever-present guitar. Thanksgiving poured out to the Savior as they recounted how the Lord had watched over them the past couple of years, and how he had bonded them together as a family.

Five months later (February 1981), Martha felt comfortable enough to write a prayer letter to their team members back home, bearing only her newly acquired signature of "Martha Foulkes."

*We had a good month with Jackie at home for her Christmas holidays. I was able to be off work for the whole month, and that made it possible for us to spend more time together. Jackie helped with all of the Christmas preparations, and I taught her to drive the car.*

Martha still had to do a balancing act with her part-time teaching and administrative duties at the nursing school and the demands of being a homemaker. "We praise the Lord for the strength and wisdom He gave when Martha was being pulled in several different directions," Jim commented.

The Foulkes home was still the first stop for many visitors and dignitaries passing through. (There were no roadside inns nor motels.) Sometimes uninvited guests arrived at early morning hours, tired and weary, just looking for a place to crash. Martha and the rest of the family made them all feel wanted and welcome.

In May of 1982, nurse Marie Collins came back from furlough and took over the reins of the nursing school, easing the load for Martha, which was a welcome change.

The year 1982 was the first furlough for Martha as a member of the Foulkes family. And it would be an eventful year for all. Gwennie graduated from Columbia Bible College in June; Terrie represented the family for that occasion.

Jackie graduated from Rift Valley Academy in Kenya in July. Jim gave the graduation address—but not before he took time out to climb nearby Mt. Kenya a few days earlier. The whole family had somehow managed to be there to cheer Jackie on as she accepted her diploma. Jackie chose to follow her father and sister Terrie by going to Asbury College in the Kentucky bluegrass area. Terrie moved from

South Carolina to work in a hospital in nearby Lexington, so she could provide some family support for her little sister.

Jim and Martha arrived in North America in August of 1982. A great deal of the time was spent in border hopping. Most of Martha's relatives, friends, and supporters lived in Canada; while most of Jim's were in the States. For the first time, Martha would learn how to live out of a suitcase. They would travel twenty-two thousand miles on furlough, permitting Martha to see thirty-two U.S. states for the first time.

The couple found, however, that North America has its hazards as well as Africa—though of an entirely different kind. Their close call with death took place in the Canadian Rockies as they were coming out of a tunnel in a high pass. Jim accounted the accident in a newsletter dated February 1983:

Have you ever heard of black ice? Its most distinctive feature is that it has no glare and is virtually invisible—only the black top underneath can be seen. The effect of the ice was felt only after I had unwisely elected to overtake a slow-moving car. After some fancy figure skating on the ice, we headed for the scenic route— the downside of the mountain.

A guard rail intercepted us and, even though we sheared off twenty feet of the rail, it kept us on the road. The front two feet of the car were destroyed, but we hardly felt anything.

I hopped out of the car to see our battery still speeding down the highway like a hockey puck—so much for my request to Martha to put on the hazard lights.

We were so thankful for the Lord's good care of us, in particular for the overworked angels that He has commissioned to keep us from stubbing our foot.

To Jim, the incident was another "reminder that while we are in His will, we are indestructible until our work is finished. How wonderful to know that we don't have to fret over nuclear war or even drunk drivers." Or black ice or stampeding elephants.

Jim had set a medical goal for his furlough to get some experience in cataract surgery, but that began to look impossible because

*A spot of tea in the backyard.*

of the time crunch. "The Lord helped out in a manner that was unusual enough that His intervention was hard to mistake," Jim remarked.

Jim, Martha, and the girls had stopped off for the night in a motel in Minnesota. Terrie amused herself by seeing how many non-Swedish names she could find in that very Scandinavian town.

After wading through several pages of the telephone book, Terrie asked Jim: "Is Gess Swedish?"

"That wouldn't be Lowell Gess, would it?"

Terrie couldn't believe it. The first name was Lowell!

Lowell Gess was Jim's old friend from their surgical residency days in Akron, in the 1950s. Jim immediately called him. Lowell and his wife, Ruth, drove over to the motel for a happy reunion. Jim learned that Dr. Gess spent two months a year in an eye clinic in West Africa, where he did more cataract extractions in a day than he would do in a week in Minnesota. He invited Jim to spend a week with him in his eye clinic in Sierra Leone on his way back to Zambia.

Jim later wrote, "That turned out to be a great time. It was a clear picture of what a tremendous service and ministry a comprehensive eye clinic can be when the services are given in the name and love of Jesus."

Jim's keen interest in cataract surgery stemmed from two sources—one spiritual and the other physical. The fact that so many of the recorded healings by the Lord were to restore sight illustrated His special compassion for the blind. The Lord Himself described His own mission as "preaching the gospel to the poor, healing the brokenhearted, preaching deliverance to captives and *recovery of sight* . . ." (Luke 4:18, author's emphasis).

Jim had long been frustrated in seeing how few of the old cataract-blinded patients in Zambia were able to make the long trip to town for surgery. He was ecstatic when he had the opportunity of helping his first cataract-blinded patient to see in the name of Jesus.

Jim quickly pointed out to the doctors who received his prayer letter that they would realize more than others how impossible it is to compress a multi-year residency into two weeks, but "that was all the time I had." (Jim received his second week of training, along with Martha, at the Africa Evangelical Fellowship [AEF] sister hospital at Luampa.) He did eighteen cataract extractions there under the supervision of doctors Gordon Jones and Milan Springle.

The fact that Martha trained alongside him as a scrub nurse was a real bonus. "A specially trained scrub nurse is a very vital part of successful eye surgery, and it has been fun to work with Martha on this joint project."

*This old blind couple had been abandoned by their village. They didn't hesitate about going to the hospital for cataract surgery; they would have gone anywhere for some food.*

# All Healing Is God's

When the whirlwind residency was over, there was no choice but to take the plunge and start the program at Mukinge, knowing that every person that was being operated on would never see again if that opaque lens was not removed. "That knowledge gave me the courage to begin even with such limited training," Jim concluded.

Jim and Martha were now on their own at Mukinge. The first few cases were very carefully chosen since just one catastrophe would shut down the eye program. That didn't happen.

Jim believed that the One who called him to be a medical missionary would give him all the gifts needed to accomplish that goal. He was highly motivated and willing to take risks—whether in the hospital with a scalpel or with a gun in the jungle.

It soon became obvious that Jim would never have the opportunity of helping the great majority of blind people by just waiting on them to come to the hospital. Generally considered of little value to the village community, the blind were not important enough for others to expend the effort to get them to Mukinge. "We soon realized that we had to go find them in their villages," Jim stated.

Many helping hands pitched in to get the eye program up and running. The German eye mission (C.B.M.) supplied eye drugs, and paid for an optical workshop where affordable glasses were assembled for the needy. The Canadian eye mission (Operation Eye Sight Universal, or O.E.U.), kindly agreed to fund a vehicle for the mobile eye clinic, supplied the wages for the eye staff, and also funded housing for an ophthalmic-trained clinical officer.

The clinical officer who came to live in that house was a very special person chosen by God. Jairos Fumpa was at the very top of his class at the Clinical Officer Training College in Lusaka. Upon graduation, he felt as clearly called to come to Mukinge as any missionary would have.

Soon after arriving, he was sent to Malawi for a one-year eye course and graduated number one in his class. Later, he completed a course in the U.K. on administration and, more recently, a two-year eye surgery course in Malawi, that made him a fully qualified eye surgeon.

Jairos was the backbone of the eye program since the beginning, and he is the hope of the future. He told Jim a number of

*Jairos Fumpa and Maybin returning three post-op cataract patients to their homes. A year later, the hospital began placing intra-ocular lenses and dispensed with the heavy glasses with which these ladies are burdened.*

times "Uncle, the first day I arrived here I told you that I was going to stay here until I retire, and that is still my commitment."

Another move forward was the addition of an operating microscope that allowed the use of intraocular lenses (IOLs). "Saying good-bye to the thick 'coke-bottle' lenses that were required post op was a great advance," Jim added. The IOLs couldn't get scratched, lost, or sat upon like the thick, heavy cataract glasses. Jim smiled as he remembered, "It was amusing to see one of my early patients who had tied his post op specs on topside down since the lower half of the lens was too scratched to see through." The IOLs put an end to problems like that.

Jim added, "It was pure joy to see the faces of the patients when the first dressings were removed after their operations. As light flooded into their eyes, some cried, some reached out to touch me, or to point to the nurse." There was invariably profuse thanks. Jim stated, "That was my opportunity to point their praise to the One in whose name we had prayed before surgery and Who had called me to follow in His footsteps to recover sight for the blind."

Visiting each of the thirteen rural health centers in the district, the Mukinge eye team would always fill up the back of the pickup truck with people who needed surgery at the hospital. On one visit the team was directed to an old blind couple who were virtually abandoned. The rest of the village had moved a mile away to tend their gardens and left the blind couple to fend for themselves. In pitiful shape, and having not eaten for days, the couple was easily persuaded to allow the team to take them to the hospital. They would have gone anywhere just to get some food, the prospect of eye surgery was a secondary benefit. They soon regained their strength from the nourishment of the food and then received their sight back after cataract surgery. Jim concluded, "Rather than just saving their eyes, I'm rather certain that their lives were saved as well, and they gave God the glory."

In latter days, the eye program has been able to reach more cataract-blinded people using the skills of Jim's son-in-law, Don Amborski. Don was able to fly the eye team to distant hospitals for two days of eye surgery, eventually adding five other hospitals where extractions were performed. That helped hundreds of other people to see each year. After Jim retired, Dr. Bob Wenninger expertly carried on the entire eye program until his own retirement. Jairos Fumpa, fully certified as an eye surgeon, carries on the complete program with great skill to this day.

"Helping the blind to see in Jesus' name was undoubtedly the most rewarding part of missionary medicine," Jim said, looking back on it all. "I am so thankful that the Lord allowed me that opportunity." Jim reveled in the wonder-working power of God, that He could take a simple act like looking up a name in a phone book in Minnesota, and use it as a first link in a long chain of events to bring healing to the blind in Zambia.

Vision is such a precious faculty; we often take it for granted. Not so Jim, as he recalled one of the most amazing stories of medical miracles. It happened to a Catholic missionary friend of his, who had an accident, seriously damaging his eyes.

Father Terry was assigned to the Northwestern Province in the early 1970s, and used to travel to Kasempa, near Mukinge, for a day or two each month, to visit the small handful of Catholic adherents.

After becoming acquainted with Jim, the two men found that they had much in common. Terry was from Kenton, Ohio, not far from Lima. They both had graduated from high school the same year and had come to Zambia as missionaries at almost the same time. Terry often shared meals with the Foulkes family.

One fateful night, Terry was driving with a friend on the primitive back road through the Kafue National Park. Because it was getting late, they decided to camp along the Lunga River for the night. Unfortunately, Terry's flashlight batteries were almost dead. A game ranger had told him that dead batteries could be recharged by simply placing them near the coals of a campfire, so Terry decided to test the ranger's theory.

After several minutes, Terry noticed that one battery had already begun to bubble from the intense heat. He took a stick to flick the battery out of the bed of coals. When the stick poked the battery, it exploded, blowing hot metal fragments into both of his eyes. Fearing the worst—blind for life—and suffering excruciating pain, Terry knew that he had to get to a hospital fast. And that would be Mukinge—ninety miles away over terrible roads.

His companion couldn't drive, and the limited vision that Terry had left allowed him only to differentiate between light and dark. The road was a little lighter than the bush. With his friend playing the role of seeing-eye dog, Terry drove slowly toward Mukinge.

On several occasions the constant pain surged, nearly causing him to pass out. It was a terrific test of endurance, taking them almost all night to drive the ninety miles of bone-jarring, pockmarked roads.

As soon as they arrived at the Mukinge hospital, Jim rushed Terry to the operating room and put him to sleep. He then inserted lid retractors to get his first look at the priest's eyes. Metallic fragments had splattered his corneas, some very deep and on the verge of penetrating all the way through. Jim knew that the deep wounds would scar and cause multiple opacities, leaving Terry functionally blind for life.

After a full hour of carefully picking out the metallic fragments with the aid of a strong operating-room light and a magnifying loupe, Jim applied antibiotic ointment and atropine to keep his pupils dilated. As he bandaged his friend's eyes, Jim was sure his friend would be blind.

When Terry woke up following surgery, he immediately asked: "Will I be blind?"

Jim swallowed hard, knowing that this wasn't the time to answer in the affirmative. He assured him that he would be better able to evaluate his eyes on the second day, and would give him an honest appraisal then.

The first day, Jim changed the dressings and applied more ointment but didn't examine the eyes closely, afraid of what he might discover.

On the second day, as he slowly removed the bandages, he did a quick double take. He couldn't believe what he was seeing. A more careful examination revealed the unbelievable. There was no pitting at all of Terry's corneal surfaces! None!

Jim said, "By all the laws of nature, it was too soon for those defects to have healed, and there was not a sign of opacification! God had simply reversed the natural course of those severely injured eyes."

Jim didn't have to tell his friend that he could see; Terry knew that by the fact that he could clearly see the tears streaming down Jim's face. His vision was 100 percent and, what's just as amazing, he had no pain at all!

"There was now nothing to do but to bow in reverential awe to the Light of the World for His goodness in granting this miracle. It was time to thank the Lord—which we did profusely!" Jim exclaimed.

Jim recalled the words of Dr. Bob Foster, who often said: "The miraculous usually occurs when God wants to authenticate His Word or His work. All healing is God's."

Father Terry wrote of this against-all-natural-order experience to his family and friends, giving God the glory. As a result, Mukinge Hospital received gifts totaling several thousand dollars from the grateful family and friends.

Jim said, "I didn't ask the Lord to make my friend Terry to see again. My faith was too small to take a leap like that. God's ways are mysterious. For His own reasons, the Lord touched Father Terry's eyes with the healing hands that had made so many blind people see when He walked on the earth."

The Lord "is the same yesterday and today and forever" (Heb. 13:8 NIV).

# ChapterTwenty-eight
## AIDS Comes to Mukinge

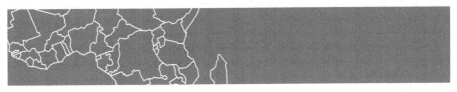

Soon after Jim and Martha returned to Mukinge and the eye program was getting underway, their lives and the lives of those all around them were affected by the beginning trickles of what has become a veritable flood, a catastrophe of generational proportions.

Jim's patient was a woman in her early twenties. She had been sick for some time before she arrived at Mukinge. It fell to Jim to tell her that she had only a few weeks to live, the first firmly diagnosed case of AIDS at Mukinge. The year was 1986.

"I was surprised when she said that she knew of the disease called AIDS, since very few of the people in our area at that time had even heard of it," Jim said.

She admitted that she had been a prostitute in Lusaka (the capital), and that four of her friends had died of the "slim" disease—the African name for AIDS because the patients lose so much weight. She recognized those same symptoms in her own body.

Tears swelled up and rolled down her face as the reality of her imminent death sank in.

The young, doomed patient heard the bad news in July of that year. Two days later, she heard the good news of the gospel of Jesus Christ, and confessed her sins to the One who could forgive her and grant her eternal life.

Jim said, "The Lord dried this young woman's tears and gave her the assurance that even though her earthly body had only a few days to live, she was going to live forever with the Lord. What a fantastic swap."

Jim was among more than a hundred physicians who had attended a refresher course in Kenya the preceding year of 1985. Professor Rick Goodgame, an internationally known expert on AIDS, who was working in AIDS-stricken Uganda, was a featured speaker. Looking across a group of doctors from nearly every nation on the African continent, Dr. Goodgame asked, "How many of you have ever diagnosed a case of AIDS?"

Not a single hand went up.

Obviously surprised at the lack of hands, Dr. Goodgame uttered these chilling words: "We will meet again in two years, and by then every single one of you will have entered the AIDS era."

His prediction was totally on target.

By the end of 2004, the Joint United Nations Programme on HIV/AIDS (UNAIDS) estimated that sub-saharan Africa had twenty-five million cases of HIV/AIDS with 2.3 million having died.

The HIV/AIDS firestorm also engulfed Zambia. The prevalence rate in 2004 was 26 percent for urban dwellers from fifteen to forty-nine years of age. A fifteen-year-old boy in Zambia had a 75 percent chance of dying of AIDS.

Zambian vice president Nevers Mumba highlighted the immense sociological tragedy of AIDS when he told the *New York Times*, "We spend all this time training people and by the time they get to the first tier of their careers we are ready to bury them."

*Kingsley giving an AIDS prevention lecture to a grade school. All the primary and secondary schools in the district were visited once a year.*

220

# AIDS Comes to Mukinge

Jim believed that the earliest AIDS patients at Mukinge—sometime in the mid–1980s—were misdiagnosed. "We probably diagnosed them as fever of undetermined origin, or perhaps chronic liver disease. Presumptive diagnosis is a good cover term that sometimes allows us doctors to hide behind our own ignorance," he said candidly.

Early on, the question "Where and when did the HIV virus start?" was so fraught with political overtones, that the medical side of the question often got lost. At several early international AIDS conferences where the papers presented ended up pointing the finger at Africa, some of the offended African delegates promptly walked out.

The subject was considered politically incorrect and not allowed on the agenda again. It also could be bad for the economy. A high incidence of AIDS is hard on tourism. In Africa, it was also hard on pride. Often, relatives would (unsuccessfully) try to bribe Jim to delete the word AIDS on the death certificate of their loved one.

Militant Africans blamed the "gay plague" on promiscuous homosexual Americans. The Americans returned the favor by blaming Africa and Haiti. The big difference in Africa, where homosexuality is almost taboo, is that AIDS is largely a heterosexually transmitted disease.

Jim said matter of factly, "Without question, the epicenter of the pandemic (AIDS) began in an area including Uganda and Northeastern Congo." But it spread in a deadly walk down the continent of Africa, where 60 percent of all sufferers in the world with HIV/AIDS live. Jim believes:

> What we are in, really, is a war. A war against AIDS. Almost daily we would be faced with a young child who was failing to thrive. A blood test would confirm that the child was HIV positive and almost certainly would be dead within six months. The parents (who very often were as yet symptom free) had to be informed. They, of course, received the dreaded news with great sorrow, knowing that as well as losing this child, their older children would almost surely become orphans.

Tuberculosis and HIV often rode in tandem. An adult admitted to the Mukinge Hospital TB ward in those early days

*Sharing the gospel with an AIDS patient. He weighed only ninety-five pounds.*

had more than a 60 percent chance of being HIV positive. An all-out effort was made to move the AIDS cases out as quickly as possible. Otherwise, all of the adult wards would be filled beyond capacity, leaving no beds for newly diagnosed cases who were waiting to be admitted.

Furthermore, the tainting of the blood supply with HIV placed anyone getting a blood transfusion at high risk of contracting HIV. No longer did the rapid life-saving benefits of transfusion (such as in cases of trauma resuscitation) outweigh the risk of a hopeless scenario of the patient slowly dying of AIDS.

The transfusion problem is highlighted by a story Jim tells of a close friend, the local police chief, who had contracted HIV and was slowly dying of AIDS. He wanted to get to his home in another province to die, but he could not make the long trip without a blood transfusion. And that posed a problem.

"I asked him to send over four of his constables so that we could check their suitability as blood donors. All four were HIV positive. I realized it was probably futile to check the rest of the force," Jim said.

The police chief finally was able to find an "old auntie" whose blood passed the HIV test. The chief then was able to survive the long bumpy road home so he could be buried with his ancestors.

Jim remembered, "For a time, more policemen in Zambia were dying of AIDS than could be replaced by the training programs."

Ironically, it was Uganda, the country initially with the highest incidence of AIDS, which provided the most successful model for confronting the killer disease. The country sponsored a nation-wide "ABC" campaign—Abstain, Be faithful, or as a last resort, use a Condom.

Churches and mosques, as well as clinics and public schools, were involved in the anti-AIDS crusade. Religious leaders joined government officials in spreading the message: abstain from sex before marriage and be faithful to your partner after marriage.

The Ugandan program went against the grain of the international AIDS establishment which emphasized "safe" sex, i.e., use of a condom. But in Uganda, the emphasis was on abstinence rather than relying on condoms.

Ugandan president, Yoweri Museveni, flat-out rejected the Western priority of condom distribution—as if "only a thin piece of rubber stands between us and the death of our continent."

The godly first lady of Uganda, Jane Museveni, traveled to every district of the country urging everyone to follow the ABC pattern. This emphasis reduced the national infection rate from 21 percent to 6 percent among pregnant mothers, and in Kampala (the capital), the rate dropped from 30 percent to 10 percent. There is no other success story like that in the world.

At Mukinge, Jim and his surgeon colleague Dr. Bob Wenninger assumed responsibility for counseling all newly diagnosed HIV patients. They quickly set up a protocol. They would allocate fifteen minutes for the bad news, explaining the disease, and answering questions. This was then followed by giving fifteen minutes of the good news of the gospel. As a result, many of the young people diagnosed with the fatal disease turned to the Savior and accepted His offer of eternal life.

Seeing the devastation AIDS was causing, Jim became more and more involved in the areas of education and prevention. He lectured on the new plague at adult church conferences, choir conferences, and to the high schools in the district. "I spent a lot of time talking about the consequences of sexual immorality, which in the case of AIDS, meant death," Jim said.

Once the hospital obtained its own HIV testing kits, the number of fresh cases diagnosed ballooned alarmingly. The additional time needed for counseling placed a heavy burden on both Jim and Bob.

With AIDS on the rampage, filling the hospital wards to overflowing and causing caretakers to suffer burn-out every year or two, the medical staff at Mukinge decided it was time to develop an AIDS team. Finding the right people to run such a program was vital. It became obvious to Jim that God's hand was directing the recruiting of the fledgling AIDS team.

The first man to come aboard was a devout Christian, Kingsley Kuwema, a three-year-trained clinical officer. Kingsley had been assigned by the Zambian Ministry of Health to work at a government hospital 160 miles west of Mukinge. Upon hearing of the need for someone to work full time with AIDS patients at Mukinge, Kingsley was convinced that the Lord had prepared and then called him to fill the position.

"What a jewel he has been. He gets so much satisfaction from leading AIDS patients to the Lord during his counseling sessions that he doesn't get depressed. He is by far the longest serving AIDS worker in Zambia," Jim said.

To round out the AIDS team, an experienced public health nurse was needed. Once again, the Lord filled the need in the person of Jean Williams, who had been serving as a public health nurse for AEF in Gabon. A self-starter, she immediately took over the Mukinge AIDS program, introducing many creative and useful ideas along the way.

Kingsley and Jean became even more invaluable after attending training sessions on home-based care at Chikankata Hospital in the Southern Province. The hospital developed a model that would be used all over Africa.

The plan called for a short admission to the hospital if inpatient care was required. The secondary diseases associated with HIV infection are treated while the patient is in the hospital. Following the treatment, the patient is discharged. Then home-based care begins.

But for the AIDS team to get to the homes, transport was required. *Jehovah-Jireh* (God provides) once again filled the need. The Scandinavians were donating money to hospitals interested in

# AIDS Comes to Mukinge

*Kingsley, Jean, and Daisy visit an AIDS client in his village to give him encouragement, spiritual counsel, and any helpful medicine. The ears of the patient's fellow villagers are wide open to hear the message of AIDS prevention that the team will give.*

follow-up care of AIDS patients in the home setting. A Norwegian donor agency gave the hospital enough money to purchase a vehicle and maintain it, thereby permitting the AIDS team to visit every patient at home at least once a month.

During the home visits, the team gave medicine to treat any new diseases, and provided blankets or clothes as needed. This gave team members an opportunity to encourage the patients and their families. As many of the AIDS patients had become Christians during their stay at the hospital, they appreciated prayer and readings from the Scriptures.

Hospital chaplains joined the team as needed. The pre-test HIV counseling, as well as the post-test counseling, kept the team members busy at the hospital. But they still managed to visit more than two hundred outpatient clients monthly in their scattered home villages.

"It is a rare day for the team if they don't have the opportunity to lead at least one AIDS sufferer to new life in Christ," Jim said.

And they were making a difference: the most recent large study at Mukinge's antenatal department revealed that the number of expectant mothers who are HIV positive has dropped from 14 percent to 11 percent—a significant reduction.

Jim said, "It has been very rewarding to the AIDS prevention staff to realize that twelve years of hard work has finally reversed the annual increase in mothers who are HIV infected. How encouraging to prove that as followers of Jesus we really do have the answer to winning the AIDS war."

# ChapterTwenty-nine
## Fast Forward to Good-bye, Zambia

Too quick the years. Too short the days. Too sudden the end. The old jungle doctor of seventy summers was headed toward the finish line of retirement. He would hang up his stethoscope and lay down his scalpel on January 1, 1997, after thirty-eight years in the front lines of medical mission work, caring for the sick and injured.

Jim Foulkes was leaving his home sweet home—Mukinge.

He was leaving the house that he had helped design, and where his children had grown up. He had to bid a sad farewell to the hospital which he had seen grow from a somewhat primitive sixty-bed rural place of healing to a two-hundred-bed referral hospital.

It was also a time for reflection.

Jim derived more genuine satisfaction from teaching TEE (Theological Education by Extension) classes for twenty-five years than any other spiritual endeavor.

He recalled how he and Marilynn, equipped with the first TEE book freshly translated into Kikaonde, set out in their old Land Rover to Nyoka, seventy miles from Mukinge. They had to pass five local churches on the way. The leaders of those congregations hopped on board, so the class ended up with fifteen students. Twelve of them finished nine courses taught over three years. During the rainy season, arriving at the class sometimes required shoring up a collapsed bridge or cording a swampy section with logs.

In his last TEE class, there were seventeen students representing the deacons and elders of seven churches. The Bible truths taught in that class would be passed on to hundreds of other Christians. He believed his time spent with TEE was his finest hour. And the blessings just kept on going.

For Martha, it was the end of twenty-five years of service as a teaching and practicing nurse. She moved out of her principal

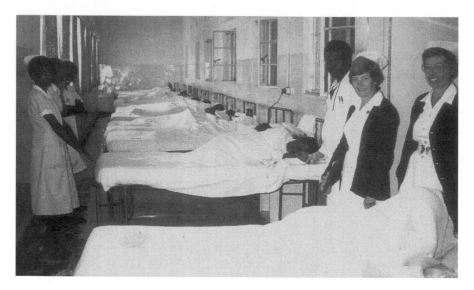

*The wards were polished and waiting for national examiners to arrive and give a practical exam to our senior finalists. Ellen Waldock and Martha don't look worried since they taught the students well.*

tutor's office in September of '96 and handed over the position to Ellen Waldock, who was ably assisted by Mary Arnold.

Martha continued in the training school, however, until the end of the year. That gave her a gentle move out of the school where she had ministered for most of her twenty-five years at Mukinge. The fifteen students who had just written their final exams expressed their gratitude to the departing teacher with a special dinner and a program. She was also honored at the New Year's watch night service.

In fact, both Jim and Martha spent their last days at Mukinge attending farewell parties and dinners, including a four-and-a-half-hour program with several hundred church representatives from all over the district, and a dinner with the entire senior staff at the hospital (including the paramount chief of the Kaonde tribe).

Perhaps the most emotional affair took place in the secondary school auditorium, when about three hours into the program, everyone there was given the opportunity to come forward and give Jim and Martha a hug and a final word. Tears flowed and tissues were at a premium.

Jungle Jim also felt sad about saying farewell to the huge herds of wild game in the Kafue National Park. On one of his recent visits,

Jim and his family witnessed a cheetah making a kill after patiently stalking a herd of Letchwe antelope. It was a scene right out of a *National Geographic* film special.

"Wild Africa always had a strong attraction for me, and a safari with a camera or a gun, when collecting meat for the hospital or our own pot, was always exciting. Sitting up in a tree stand with a bow in retirement just doesn't compare," he said.

On March 1, 1997, Jim and Martha, with Doraine Ross and Keith and Ann Donald, began a slow safari driving down to Capetown. Martha had never visited some of the jewels of Southern Africa, so this was her chance to see the impressive Eastern Highlands of Zimbabwe and the spectacular Garden Route of the east coast of South Africa, plus the beautiful city of Capetown.

Jim had some hesitation about returning to Capetown. He had not been in that city since the memorial service for Marilynn twenty years before. He knew that one of the main highways they would be traveling on passed right by the huge hospital where Marilynn had died. He had some concern that seeing the hospital again might evoke some of the sad emotions connected to Marilynn's death and would come back to haunt him.

As they passed the hospital, Jim took a long hard look. He couldn't believe it. He had no memory at all of the sadness and overwhelming grief he had experienced when Marilynn died. He only relived something of the glorious Presence of the living Lord who comforted him in that desperate time.

Jim looked slowly over at Martha, with a smile on his face and love in his heart. It was indeed well with his soul.

"Magnify the Lord with me, and let us exalt His Name forever" (Ps. 34:3).

# Epilogue

**M**artha and I retired to Boone, North Carolina, and we love living in the mountains with wonderful friends. Our church has given us many opportunities to use our gifts and experiences.

Terrie and her husband, Ian Caisley, live near Lake Erie in New York State, where Ian practices medicine and Terrie keeps busy by home schooling our grandchildren Colin and Madelynn and helping with the practice. They are very active in their church, and Ian reaches out to his patients with the touch of Christ.

Gwen serves with Serving in Mission (SIM) at Mukinge, where she was born, and has a ministry of music in the churches. Her husband, Don Amborski, has also followed in his father's footsteps as the mission pilot. Their children, Jamie, Raymond, and Marilynn, love growing up in Africa just like their parents.

Jackie and her husband, Mark Royster, are serving in Kenya, where Mark loves teaching the next generation of African church leaders at the Nairobi Evangelical Graduate School of Theology. Jackie is busy and happy entertaining and home schooling their children Helene, Daniel, and Emily.

## ROCKING CHAIR?

Leaving Africa in 1997, we knew that we would be moving to Boone, thanks to the kindness of Dr. and Mrs. Dick Furman, who were providing us with a free retirement home. My cousin, John Foulkes, wrote to our family and supporters to raise enough money for us to buy a good used car. At the end of a career with a faith mission, those two needed items are not part of the "contract," and we all have the privilege of watching the Lord meet those needs.

Living with the Blue Ridge Parkway right in front of our home, and having seventy empty acres behind us, is about as ideal a place to retire as one could ever dream. It was certainly beyond any dream that we had. It was now time to find some friends and make a new life.

We were far from our daughters and their families, and far from the Mukinge missionary family where we had been so closely connected. We missed the joy of just dropping in on a friend for a cuppa (tea) without making any prior arrangements—almost impossible in busy America. We soon realized that we were lonely, and asked the Lord to connect us with some more friends.

Three months into our retirement, we attended the Alliance Bible Fellowship. An elder invited us to eat lunch with his family that Sunday noon and then to visit their small group that evening. At the end of that evening, we both knew that we had arrived. We never looked back. Thank you, Lord!

*Jim and Martha's hut at Lui Hospital in Southern Sudan, 1998. A bomb shelter was located approximately ten feet away.*

# Epilogue

## RETURN TO AFRICA

When I laid aside my stethoscope at Mukinge, I never expected to practice medicine again. When we said good-bye to our Zambian friends at the various farewell parties, it was especially sad since we were sure that at our next meeting we would be in heaven.

The World Medical Mission (an arm of Samaritan's Purse) is located on the same road on which our house sits. The director, Robert Bell, had visited us at Mukinge, and we deepened our friendship now that we lived in Boone.

Robert was looking for doctors to help staff Lui Hospital, a medical work in war-torn Southern Sudan that Samaritan's Purse had recently resurrected. Robert contacted Martha and I and dangled a veritable carrot. If we would serve for two months at Lui, he would also include a ticket to Zambia. That was irresistible, since we could visit Gwen and her family at Mukinge. Time to dust off the stethoscope.

The African wars had been waged all around Zambia in all four directions, but we were a protected island. So going to a war zone was different for Martha and me. Anytime the drone of an airplane sounded in the sky, everything stopped until the plane could be identified. The Russian Antonov bombers used by the Muslim North had a distinctive sound, and the old-timers could easily identify them from far away. We had a bomb shelter ten feet in front of our hut, and evidence suggested that we might have to use it. There were over fifty bombed-out craters pockmarking the perimeter around the hospital where the Northern government had tried to destroy it.

Heavy rains had put two feet of green, foul water in the shelter, and Martha and I made up our minds that we would take our chances just lying flat on the ground if and when the bombs fell.

The Muslim North had infiltrated the area several years ago and, when finally driven out, left behind some parting gifts to be remembered by—hundreds and hundreds of land mines. The grass fires that spread in the dry season had already detonated scores of the mines, but, needless to say, we religiously stayed on the main road and major trails.

While repairing a patient's hernia one morning, a huge thunderous roar broke the silence and the floor shook. Our first thought was *bomb*. Then, we quickly put in some skin staples and ran to the overhanging rock that was the nearest bomb shelter. We soon found out that the culprit was a land mine detonating and not a bomb. Two herd boys were tending their cows close to the hospital, and one of them foolishly kicked a piece of metal. Fortunately, neither boy suffered fatal injuries.

Our mission was to heal the bodies of the poor in Jesus' name. It was a great thrill to wield the scalpel again. I was back doing what I was meant to be doing. The solar lights in the operating room in Sudan burned many an evening for emergency surgery. We treated some war-related injuries, but the bulk of the operations consisted of hernia repairs. Some days we would see at least six new hernia sufferers, and we had over one hundred people with hernias already on the list waiting under a tree, hoping their names would be called for admission. The size of some of the hernias was shocking, and I snapped a picture of one patient just to prove that, with scrotal extension, they can hang all the way to the knee.

Anglican missionaries arrived here just after World War I, and they established a very strong church in this large area. The

*Daughter Terrie with her husband, Ian Caisley, and their children, Madelynn and Colin.*

# Epilogue

*Daughter Gwen with her husband, Don Amborski, and their children, Raymond, Jamie, and Marilynn.*

hospital was founded early in the work since the pioneer was a doctor. The "Silent Holocaust," as the present world's longest-lasting war is correctly called, forced the closure of the hospital. It was not reopened until Samaritan's Purse took it over.

The mission station is in a very strategic area. Reopening the hospital and starting food and seed distribution for the district was a terrific help to this war-ravaged land. When Franklin Graham visited the hospital while we were there, the people turned out in the thousands to welcome him and thank him for turning their lives around. It was the greatest outpouring of thankfulness that I have ever witnessed. Franklin was careful to assure everyone that this aid did not come from him or his organization, but from the good hand of God Himself, who had instructed them to come and help in the name of Jesus.

One of the local church leaders said it well, "We have nothing, but we have everything." The war had driven them from their homes repeatedly, their crops had been burned, and their cattle killed, and some had even been sold into slavery, but they had held onto their Christian faith. They had found the pearl of great price and, therefore, they had everything of eternal value.

As well as two visits to Sudan, we also had the treat of going back to Mukinge for three months. What a joy to return to the wonderful "rut," and to work again with the special people who had been so important in our lives.

Then our sister hospital at Luampa sent an SOS for help, and we were glad to answer the call twice. Out of the five tribal languages spoken at Luampa, I could understand only one, so a translator was a necessity. He tagged along with me all day long, and he was especially helpful in the afternoon when I was doing minor surgery since he was the only one available to hold the retractors.

Since the people at Luampa knew that I had been doing eye surgery at Mukinge, those afflicted with blindness started pouring in. That was a real problem to me since I wanted to help them, but I didn't have all of the needed instruments. Nor was there anyone on the surgical staff who had any experience in eye surgery.

One day, a lady arrived who had walked with her blind husband over one hundred miles. Her eloquent plea for help,

*Daughter Jackie with her husband, Mark Royster, and their children, Emily, Daniel, and Helene.*

made while bowing on both knees and with tears running down her cheeks, was too much, and I scheduled her husband for bilateral cataract extraction.

Even though it was a struggle to operate under such sub-optimal conditions, the man could see well post-op. The picture I have of the huge smiles on the faces of the man and his faithful wife was my reward, plus the praise that the Lord received. But, of course, once the word got around that eye surgery was again being done, it brought a fresh throng of blind people.

Each trip back to Zambia was a fresh reminder as to the devastation being caused by the runaway AIDS epidemic. It is too easy to forget what a terrible way to die it is for its victims and what a disaster for Africa. The first day back at the hospital is enough to bring you back into the discouraging world of HIV and its terrible consequences. How thankful it makes one for the Mukinge AIDS team and many more like them, who are committed to bringing loving care to the victims and their families, plus the hope of eternal life.

Looking back, I can't think of a calling that would compare with the great joy and satisfaction that I have had as a medical missionary. I guess my mother was right when she taught me as a young man: "If God calls you to be a missionary, don't stoop to become the president."

# Selected Reading

Information on the history of Mukinge Hill Station is based on Dr. Bob Foster's 1990 biography, *Sword and Scalpel*, written by Lorry Lutz and published by Promise Publishing, Inc., Orange, California.

Bayly, Joseph. *The View from a Hearse*. Elgin, Ill.: David C. Cook Publishing Co., 1969.

Brand, Paul and Philip Yancey. *Fearfully and Wonderfully Made*. Grand Rapids, Mich.: Zondervan Publishing House, 1980.

Brand, Paul and Philip Yancey. *In His Image*. Grand Rapids, Mich.: Zondervan Publishing House, 1984.

Burkitt, Denis. *Eat Right to Stay Healthy and Enjoy Life More*. New York: Arco Publishing, 1979.

Elliot, Elizabeth, ed. *The Journals of Jim Elliot*. Old Tappan, N.J.: F. H. Revell Co., 1978.

Lewis, C. S. *A Grief Observed*. New York: Bantam, 1976.

Lewis, C. S. *God in the Dock*. Grand Rapids, Mich.: William B. Eerdmans Publishing, 1970.

Marshall, Catherine. *Something More*. New York: Avon Books/McGraw-Hill Book Co., 1974.

Richardson, Don. *Peace Child*. Ventura, Calif.: Regal Books, 1974.